Antony Todd is Senior Lecturer in Film Studies at the London College of Communication, University of the Arts, London.

For Rachael and Eleanor
With all my love

AUTHORSHIP
AND THE FILMS OF
DAVID LYNCH

*aesthetic receptions
in contemporary Hollywood*

ANTONY TODD

Published in 2012 by I.B.Tauris & Co Ltd
6 Salem Road, London W2 4BU
175 Fifth Avenue, New York NY 10010
www.ibtauris.com

Distributed in the United States and Canada Exclusively by Palgrave Macmillan
175 Fifth Avenue, New York NY 10010

ISBN: 978 1 84885 579 3   (HB)
          978 1 84885 580 9   (PB)

A full CIP record for this book is available from the British Library
A full CIP record is available from the Library of Congress

Library of Congress Catalog Card Number: available

Printed and bound in Great Britain by T.J. International, Padstow, Cornwall

Contents

List of Illustrations   vii

Acknowledgements   ix

Introduction   1

1. Towards a Textual Historicity   7

2. David Lynch: The Making of a
    Post-classical Auteur   14

3. Meanings and Authorships in *Dune*   38

4. Critical Theory and 'Cruel Jokes':
    Principles of Ethics and Pleasure, and
    the Reception of *Blue Velvet*   64

5. *Twin Peaks*: The Rise and Fall of a
    Public Auteur   86

6. Brand Lynch   108

7. Receiving *Mulholland Dr.*: 'A
    Contemporary Film Noir Directed
    by David Lynch'   133

Conclusion   154

Notes   157

Bibliography   163

Index   173

List of Illustrations

Eraserhead: 'A dream of dark and troubling things'   17

The Elephant Man promotional poster   27

Blue Velvet promotional poster   30

Lynch publicity portrait for *Blue Velvet*   36

Dune promotional poster   55

Lynch and MacLachlan on the set of *Blue Velvet*   59

Lynch and partner Isabella Rossellini, photographed
by Helmut Newton   84

Time, October 1990   91

Dern and Cage in *Wild at Heart*   102

Technics and American Express: auteur as product endorsement   114–15

Agent Cooper, Georgia Coffee commercial   116

Nissan Micra commercial   119

INLAND EMPIRE promotional poster   130

Mulholland Dr. promotional poster   142

Acknowledgements

This book is the outcome of many years work and I would like to thank a number of people for supporting me in my endeavours. My gratitude extends first and foremost to Pam Cook, who showed enthusiasm for this research from the beginning. Pam's support and kindness have left a lasting impression on me and this book is indebted to her wisdom. In the same breath, I would like to thank Tim Bergfelder whose attention to the fine detail of draft chapters opened up areas of important critical expansion for me. I give warm thanks to Murray Smith and Alex Neil, who provided constructive comments on draft materials and pointed me in the direction of valuable additional sources. Thanks to Colin Davies, Michael Clarke, Joel Karamath, Searle Kochberg, Valerie Swayles and Jenny Walden, who have all supported me in voice and in practical ways over the last few years. Also to Frances Clarke, Pat Fitzgerald and Philippa Brewster, who I have to thank for helping bring the manuscript up to scratch. It is inconceivable to think that this enterprise would have come together without the professional dedication of the library staff at the National Film and Television Archive, The British Library and university libraries at Southampton and Portsmouth. This project was initially funded by the Arts and Humanities Research Council and I would like to acknowledge its important role in supporting this research. Finally to my family, who have shared with me the ups and downs of completing this book. Eleanor, thanks to your fervour for all things fashion related I have remained up to speed on Lynch's excursions into this industry, and Rachael, you have lived with the texts more than anyone else. For Cecile and my Dad, both of whom have supported my endeavours and will take pride in the publication of this book. And thanks lastly, of course, to David Lynch, who prompted me to ask some questions of films to begin with.

The artist may shout from all the rooftops that he is a genius; he will have to wait the verdict of the spectators in order that this declaration take on a social value, and that, finally, posterity includes him in the primers of Art History.

Marcel Duchamp (1975: 138)

Introduction

Discussions of post-classical Hollywood cinema uniformly acknowledge the coming of the 'movie brats', a new generation of American auteurs who, at the turn of the late 1960s-early 1970s, ushered in a fresh beginning for American art films. It is within the fraternity of the 'movie brats' that David Lynch can be situated. Lynch's debut feature, *Eraserhead*, was first released in the US in 1976, although Lynch wasn't to be granted the status of auteur proper until the release of his fourth feature, and still by many accounts his masterpiece, *Blue Velvet*, in 1986. Since then, Lynch, writer/director of 10 features, and co-writer/director of the 1990s television event *Twin Peaks*, has been an enduring and high-profile figure in post-classical Hollywood, on the one hand championed as a pioneering artistic visionary who has produced 'the highest movie art... adventurous, disturbing, erotic, visually exciting and absolutely personal' (Rafferty 1990a) and, on the other, vilified for his 'stunning disregard for audience values' (Morley 1992). In the widest sense, this book takes Lynch as its subject with the goal of testing the extent to which concepts of aesthetics, authorship, originality, essence and individualism have determined the character of the promotion and reception of Lynch's films.

Given Lynch's training as a fine artist, his stated and apparent associations with avant-garde art practices and specifically his predilection for abstractions, 'dream logic' and 'paintings that move', responses to his works have tended to tempt the auteurist critic into interpretative speculations. Lynch, meanwhile, remains stubbornly disinclined to speak of causality in his films. The measure of Lynch's eminence is reflected in a number of biographies that began to emerge during the mid-to-late 1990s which have now exceeded double figures in the English language alone. Titles, including *The Film Paintings of David Lynch, Challenging Film Theory* (Mactaggart 2010); *David Lynch,*

Beautiful Dark (Olson 2008); *The Complete Lynch* (Hughes 2002); *The Passion of David Lynch* (Nochimson 1997); *Lynch on Lynch* (Rodley 1997) and *David Lynch* (Chion 1996), all recommend the textual complexities of Lynch's work and, in doing so, function to support his canonical standing as a major auteur.

There is, however, a dearth of writing on Lynch as a historically constituted agent of post-classical art cinema. This book addresses this lack in offering a historical account of Lynch's cross-media construction as a figure of notable auteurist significance. In one respect, this approach reflects something of a recent trend in auteurist criticism. Scholars such as Timothy Corrigan and Barbara Klinger offer examples of how auteurs have been thought of contextually, in Corrigan's (1998: 103) terms 'almost exclusively as publicity and advertising' and in Klinger's (1994: xii) through a case study that reconsiders 'substantially the legend of [Douglas] Sirk and his sophisticated family melodramas'. David A. Gerstner and Janet Staiger, meanwhile, edited *Authorship and Film* in 2003, an anthology that presents essays given over to 'methodological exemplars for poststructuralist authorship study', which address how the author 'functions for social action' and in the 'marking' of identities (Gerstner and Staiger 2003: Introduction). But despite these valuable developments in authorship studies, I believe there remain wider authorship concerns pertaining to the ways in which, and to whom, the author has meaning.

The above authors emerge from a critical impasse that has set history and the aesthetic text at odds even though the history of cinema can be, and in the public sphere nowadays usually is, understood as an evolutionary process. In other words, the history of cinema, like the history of art, is often explained in terms of the canons and pantheons of great films and great artists. Indeed, Andrew Sarris's essay 'The American cinema', first published in *Film Culture* in 1963, spoke of the auteur theory as 'a table of values that converts film history into directorial autobiography'. From a socio-historical point of view, such a proposition merely constitutes an imperial historicism that helps bolster the belief that the history of cinema can be understood through the remarkable deeds of 'the few brave spirits', to use Sarris's phrase (Caughie 1981: 65). We could be persuaded to follow the philosophical lead posed in the latter part of the 1960s in France by structuralism and post-structuralism and either view the author as a myth (a myth ingrained in part through the author biography) or eliminate him from the interpretive process altogether. But in doing this we would only set up a sort of three-cornered critical antagonism of which no one corner would be singularly helpful in understanding how the figure of the auteur continues to endure in the pleasure of film reception. Albeit that it was made some 30 years ago now, John Caughie's comment that, any 'attempt to move beyond auteurism […] has to recognise […] the fascination of the figure of the auteur, and the way he is used in the cinephile's pleasure' (Caughie 1981: 15), seems to me remarkably apt for the undertakings in this book.

Quite apart from seeing the auteur as unified in the first place (that is as a self-governing agent rather than a socially constituted one), the early auteurism subscribed to by Sarris, and the earlier postwar writings published through *Revue du Cinéma* and *Cahiers du Cinéma* in France, and *Movie* in the UK, were, despite not insignificant differences of opinion regarding acceptable limits for auteurist speculation, necessarily partisan. These new writings, the shared goal of which was to elevate certain popular films to the standing of art, helped secure a status for commercial cinema as an artistically credible institution, fit for more than mere entertainment.

The late 1960s marked a new dawning in the history of American cinema, a period of new Hollywood. Given the expansion of other leisure activities that occupied the time of older age groups, cinema-going became the diversion of a younger, better-educated group. The emergence of the so-called 'cine-literate generation' followed in the wake of the exhibition of European art cinemas in campus film clubs and local movie theatres, and through the emergence of taught film classes. By this time, it had become the fashion, indeed, for studios to act as distributors for European art films, which by the second half of the decade were being exhibited regularly in first run theatres. The fact that cheaply produced art cinema could prove profitable meant that studio executives were open-minded about the commercial possibilities for quickly produced art films for which they were willing to act as financiers-cum-distributors.

Closer scrutiny of histories of new Hollywood may reveal a number of precedents to be found in the earlier part of the decade. Leonard Quart and Albert Auster (1984: 68–98), for instance, discuss films produced during the early-to-mid-1960s, such as *Advise and Consent* (1962), *The Manchurian Candidate* (1962) and *The Best Man* (1964), that appealed to 'the dissenting and deviant life styles and political ideas of the young', through their 'illumination' of topics including homosexuality, racism and corruption in American politics. All the same, the generation of filmmakers who gained recognition later in the decade – the likes of Bob Rafelson, Robert Altman, Arthur Penn and Mike Nichols – represent a group of filmmakers who had begun to incorporate many of the formal devices that had been associated hitherto with the film styles of their European counterparts.

The 'movie brats', meanwhile, announced a more self-conscious second phase in new Hollywood around the turn of the decade. Film-school educated screenwriters and directors – such as Martin Scorsese, Francis (Ford) Coppola, George Lucas and Steven Spielberg – are credited with taking forward the formal techniques employed by their predecessors and contemporaries but, so it is usually argued, in a more purposeful manner. It is here that we can intersect Lynch. Thomas Elsaesser, for instance, associates Lynch with the likes of Brian De Palma, Abel Ferrara and Quentin Tarantino, in a continuum of the 'movie brat' tradition, which, as Elsaesser described it (1998: 192), rested on a critical practice that is based on 'American cinema's own understanding of itself' and which incorporates the traditions of European art cinemas tallied with a 'mixing of genres' and a 'mania for citation and self-referencing'. In Lynch's case, filmic antecedents are typically traced through European art movements – surrealism and Dada, expressionism, formalism – and, of course, American genre movies – most commonly melodrama, the crime thriller and horror.

But while Elsaesser's account offers an accurate summation of Lynch's position in these shifts, it does not allow for more nuanced engagements with the film types being produced during this period. We think of Lynch's films as art films, but the aesthetic strategies described here by Elsaesser are emblematic of a mainstream Hollywood just as much as they are of more marginal films. This proposal, the collapse of high and low culture; the blurring of aesthetic borders, is topical in discussions of postmodern cinema and Lynch's work is habitually held up as illustrative of the postmodern tendency in contemporary American cinema. Indeed, it is misleading to think industrially in terms of films being inside (mainstream) and outside (independent of) the system. At the same time, this amounts to a rather sophistic view if we are compelled, as I am, towards an understanding of the functions of the author in the selling and consumption of films.

The wider goal for this book is rooted in philosophical debates that address the manner in which cultural texts are interpreted. In this respect, my first task is to trace Lynch's career to the point at which he became a 'name'; the point at which there was industrial, critical and public agreement on what a David Lynch text should be. Indeed, when Lynch came to international public attention through the *Twin Peaks* television soap opera, the term 'Lynchian' entered the filmic vernacular as a generic signifier in its own right. The central premise, put by Wolfgang Iser (1978: 107), therefore, that in our encounters with texts there occurs a 'dynamic interaction' through which the reader '(re) constructs the aesthetic object' for themselves, is of potential value when thinking of an aesthetic interaction in which the author precedes or progresses the text. Indeed, Iser's colleague, Hans Robert Jauss (1982), with whom he emerged as a pioneering figure in the development of reception theory – *Rezeptionsäesthetik* – at the University of Konstanz (West) Germany during the 1970s and early 1980s, had argued that the reader meets the text armed with certain 'horizons of expectation', and it is in considering the manner in which those horizons are met that I believe we can begin to formulate a textual historicity.

I will explore the tenets of *Rezeptionsäesthetik* in greater depth in my first chapter, but the principle developed by Iser and Jauss would seem to be at odds with Roland Barthes's influential post-structural reflections on reading practices – 'The death of the author' (1967 (1981)), *S/Z* (1970 (1975b)) and *The Pleasure of the Text* (1973 (1975a)). Barthes famously proposed that authorial analysis be killed off (along with the critic) in a gesture that passes all hermeneutic rights to the reader. In Barthes's understanding this practice should ideally give rise to automatic, or personal, reading actions where the 'writerly' text – that is, one where meanings can be written into the text by the reader – should be set free amongst 'the infinity of languages' and thereby create infinite possibilities of connotation (Barthes 1975b: 5). Thus, while authorial analysis continues to hold sway in the public sphere, the 'death of the author' provided a catalyst for hermeneutic emancipation within critical scholarly circles.

However, the post-classical art film is a different type altogether from the auteur films of old Hollywood (even if one thinks immediately of Hitchcock and, before him, Griffith, as exempt from this rule). Under the post-classical system, the auteur is not there to be unearthed by an intellectual elite, but is nowadays prominently and publicly mediated in the promotion and critical reception of films. It would seem almost remiss, therefore, to conduct an auteurist history that does not try to account for the attitudes that promotion and criticism make manifest, and to address the role such ephemera play as dialogic go-between in the ensuing unification (or, for that matter, the alienation) of reader and text.

There are, of course, drawbacks to be negotiated in presenting such a proposition, not least the problem of the paradigmatic reader. Indeed, Barthes helped us bypass this conundrum since his call for the author's death passed hermeneutic sovereignty to the preferences of the individual. But to call for the author's death, it seems to me, is over idealistic, given the modern author's eminence in aesthetic receptions.

Historically, the inconsistency for authorship studies has been rooted in an altercation between the generic and the poetic. Although this book is an auteurist investigation, if it is to succeed in bringing anything new to the topic, then it will be necessary to think outside these limiting categories and to see Lynch's films not as essentially 'Lynchian' (although they may often be read this way), but as auteurist and generic amalgamations that are presented to us by the industry and the critic, not in some harmonious marriage of textual fixity, but as contradictory sign carriers. But to retire the author on the mutability of the sign does not take us very far in accounting for the aesthetic experience in modern film consumption. So this book will also look beyond its empiricist findings, towards the text itself, in an effort to account for the different experiences at play in the encounter between the auteurist text and the reader, and in doing so, we may (re)consider ways that the author functions for pleasure in these relationships.

CHAPTER 1

Towards a Textual Historicity

It is my intention that the chapters in this book will develop in the manner of a causal narrative. However, the methodology I have applied throughout brings together historically disparate paradigms that merit some careful negotiation. So it is to this task that we must turn in the first instance through this shorter chapter. In its rudiment, my approach brings together a contextual model, much like that applied by Klinger in her study on Douglas Sirk, and an aesthetic reception study method informed by the work of Jauss and Iser. Like Klinger (whose own research built on the work of Robert Kapsis's on Hitchcock, Jane Tompkins's on Hawthorne and Charles Masland's on Chaplin), my first aim is to offer a case study that investigates contemporaneous manners for artistic reputation building, and the standards by which those reputations are then dismantled, only, in Lynch's case, to be reassembled once more. In this regard I follow Klinger's lead when she noted that a departure 'from the idea that works alone reveal the genius of their authors ... helps us grasp the dialogic function between artistic reputations and history – the dynamic circumstances under which an author's status and the status of her or his works are established, sustained, transformed, unappreciated, or even vilified' (Klinger 1994: xiii).

Our first undertaking, then, will be to grasp the story of Lynch's passage from student filmmaker to the status of auteur proper with the release of *Blue Velvet* in 1986. Once we have established this, we will have arrived at the point at which horizons of expectation for future films 'by David Lynch' could be more or less agreed upon. We will, in other words, have set to the task of putting in place the foundations of Lynch's 'biographical legend', a hypothesis attributed initially to Boris Tomashevskii, that dates back to the early twentieth century and the literary studies conducted in the name of Russian Formalism. In his essay 'Literature and biography', Tomashevskii in some ways anticipated French structuralism by placing analytical emphasis on the texts' formal structures. Where his writing was at variance with modern rebuttals of authorship, however, was in his appreciation for the public function of the author biography. Speaking of the biography as a '*literary fact*', Tomashevskii (1971: 47–48) argued that 'we must remember that creative literature exists, not for the literary historians, but for readers, and as such, the historian 'must consider how the poet's biography operates in the reader's consciousness'.

David Bordwell applied Tomashevskii's concept in his 1988 study of Yasujiro Ozu, *Ozu and the Poetics of Cinema*. In that book, Bordwell understood the importance of the author biography in the way it permits 'works to come into being, as fulfilments of the legend; and to orient perceivers to them'. Bordwell (1988: 5–6) revealed how Ozu's legend had been built upon biographical sources that had composed 'an image [that] easily slides into the notion of Ozu the Zen artist, the simple toiler who turns out to have a deep secret'. Lynch, too, is a filmmaker concerned with secrets – what is hidden beneath surfaces – although Lynch is rather more likely to be conveyed in biographical literature as an expressionist and a surrealist; and, as personality, a rebellious eccentric who operates in defiance of the Hollywood system. These are, indeed, the principal characteristics of the horizons of expectation for films carrying Lynch's name.

But as I have said already, my field of analysis will look further than the work undertaken by Klinger and other American Reception Studies scholars, most notably at Staiger, who in her preface to *Interpreting Films*, expounded the neo-Marxist idea of a 'materialist historiography' that promotes 'contextual factors rather than textual materials or reader psychologies as most important in illuminating the reader process in interpretation' (1992: xi–xiv). While I too support the idea that understanding contextual factors is a necessity in getting to grips with what texts mean, I feel that the structural and thematic properties of poetic texts are of equal importance and must not be relegated as a result of historical imperatives. My research is not, therefore, intended to be read as a defence, or even a revised theory, of authorship. I am intent, rather, on presenting a history that takes into account the pleasure – produced through the coming together of various humanist and generic signs – that the authored text brings in the public consumption of post-classical art films.

As a means of attaining our goals, we will call upon some of the precepts of *Rezeptionsäesthetik* which, having gained recognition in the late 1960s through the research of Jauss and Iser, established its station initially within the philosophical expansion of twentieth-century literary scholarship: namely poetic formalism and linguistic theory. We know already that under the theoretical lead of post-structuralism it is usually understood that scholars will pass over the author on the grounds that hermeneutic rights reside with the reader. But through the concept of *Rezeptionsäesthetik*, and notably his 'horizons of expectation' configuration, Jauss offered us a different perspective of reception; one that is especially helpful for us given the intrusive nature of modern media systems and the way these systems construct and sustain public perceptions of the modern day auteur.

Unlike the post-structural reading model, where history becomes threatened due to the text's innumerable interpretive combinations, through the idea of an 'aesthetic of reception' Jauss proposed a critical paradigm that addresses the aesthetic perceptions of formalism while retaining a grounding in historical pragmatism. In his 1970 essay 'Literary history as a challenge to literary theory', Jauss complained that 'through their one-sidedness', Marxist and Formalist literary theories had arrived 'at an aporia' and for Jauss, any solution would demand 'that historical and aesthetic considerations be brought into a new relationship' (1982: 10). Jauss was partly critical of the Formalist method because it 'assumes that the reader has the theoretical understanding of the philologist who can reflect on the artistic devices, already knowing them', and of the Marxist school since it 'candidly equates the spontaneous experience of the reader with the scholarly interest of historical materialism, which would discover relationships between superstructure and basis in the literary work'. Jauss did not propose any kind of synthesis of the two approaches either, since this would not solve the fundamental dilemma of addressing the reader: the very person 'for whom the literary work is primarily destined'. He wrote (1982: 18–19):

> My attempt to bridge the gap between literature and history, between historical and aesthetic approaches, begins at the point [where] both schools [Marxist and Formalist] stop. Their methods conceive the literary fact

within the closed circle of aesthetics of production and of representation. In doing so, they deprive literature of a dimension that inalienably belongs to its aesthetic character as well as its social function: the dimension of its reception and influence.

Indeed, Jauss proposed that the analysis of the aesthetic experience could amount to something 'more than a simple sociology of taste', if it described:

> the reception and the influence of a work within the objectifiable system of expectations that arise for each work in the historical moment of its appearance, from a pre-understanding of the genre, from the form and themes of already familiar works, and from the opposition between poetic and practical language. (1982: 22)

Through his distinction between poetic and practical language, moreover, Jauss invokes the evaluative dichotomies that have transferred into filmic tradition through the time-honoured standoff between genre pictures and auteur pictures. Where we can start to identify cracks in the 'death of the author' approach, is in the fact that while a given text may be new to the reader (which would seem to include a text that can be theoretically happened upon, as well as a new text chosen for that which it promises to yield in terms of novelty) that text 'does not present itself as something absolutely new in an informational vacuum but predisposes its audience to a very specific kind of reception'. Indeed, Jauss suggests that the encounter with a text 'awakens memories of that which was already read, brings the reader to a specific emotional attitude, and with its beginning arouses expectations for the "middle and end," which can then be maintained intact or altered, reoriented, or even fulfilled ironically in the course of the reading according to a specific set of rules of the genre or type of text' (1982: 23). Although Jauss's proposition stands fundamentally at odds with Barthes's reading paradigm in that it supports some system for collective interpretive consciousness, his method still offers the scope to account for different textual strategies and pleasures. We know, however, that Barthes's writing addresses these ideas much less equivocally and his theory points to an elementary limitation in Jauss's model that as historians we are bound to address.

Jauss suggests that the horizon of expectation for a work 'allows one to determine its artistic character by the kind and the degree of its influence on a presupposed audience', while a change in horizons will occur when a text overrides previous expectations 'through raising newly articulated experiences to the level of consciousness'. Indeed, Jauss proposed that any new 'aesthetic distance can be objectified historically along the spectrum of the audience's reactions and criticism's judgement (spontaneous success, rejection or shock, scattered approval, gradual or belated understanding)' (1982: 25). What is of significance here is the proposition of a presupposed audience – that is for Jauss an audience that carries out 'specific instructions in a process of directed perception which can be comprehended according to its constitutive motivations and triggering signals' (1982: 23) – and the lack of the potential for discursive reading practices to come to the fore.

We find criticisms of the above in Paul de Man, who queried Jauss's 'lack of interest, bordering on outright dismissal' of the potential '"play" of the signifier' (Jauss 1982: vii–xxv); in Robert C. Holub (1984: 63), whose misgivings were directed at Jauss's tendency to 'universalize novelty' in 'determining aesthetic value'; and in Staiger (1992: 46), who believed that any emphasis on 'aesthetic horizons' would be to the 'practical neglect of discursive, social, political, and economic contexts'. In taking up these drawbacks, we should acknowledge, firstly, that Jauss's ideas were a long way removed from the context of a post-classical art cinema. Jauss was primarily concerned with the mediation of literature between past and present reading horizons (for instance, Flaubert's *Madame Bovary*, Feydeau's *Fanny* and Chateaubriand's *Atala*) (Jauss 1982: 27). But if we reposition the horizonal model in a modern filmic context I believe we are able to surmount the limitations of its literary application. There are two prevailing points that warrant our consideration in this respect.

The first of these is the objection put forward by Staiger that takes issue with any emphasis on aesthetic reception on the grounds that it is socially, politically and economically divisive (as we know, historically the business of aesthetics and poetics has tended to be administered by a cultural and intellectual elite). Indeed, Jauss was chiefly concerned with horizonal paradigms that have helped shape literary scholarships. In a filmic situation the same could be argued of auteurism, in the sense that the *Cahiers* group and their followers set about bestowing the status of artistic respectability only upon special Hollywood films. But while we would without doubt fall victim to the sort of reading snags Staiger anticipated in applying Jauss to a blanket reception study of encrypted authors in classical cinema, I believe that Jauss's ideas can be instructive if we are committed, as I am, to accounting for the sharp ascent of the modern Hollywood auteur in the public consciousness. Auteurism, in other words, has extended beyond the corral of a scholarly clique into the sphere of public discourse.

My second point relates more explicitly to the detail of the horizonal reading paradigm. It would be nonsensical to suggest that there is consensus on the merits of a given text. Lynch in particular is seen as something of an acquired taste and judgements on his films are often polarised. Additionally, we might be pressed to qualify the terms of auteurism, since its specificity as a reading paradigm is historically unstable and it has been subject to its own horizonal transformations. Paisley Livingston's comment (1997: 132) that 'it seems to be wrongly taken on faith that we [...] have a strong, shared understanding of what [the] traditional conception of authorship entails', would seem to point to a fundamental block in treating auteurism as a horizonal paradigm. Yet Livingston's thesis addresses the long succession of scholarly undertakings that have grappled with the philosophical puzzles of cinematic authorship. In the public sphere, though, there is no such authorship puzzle.

The auteurism I have in mind is identified by Staiger (2003: 30) as the 'authorship as origin approach'; an approach whereby 'the author is conceptualized as a free agent, untroubled philosophically or linguistically – although rational individuals might debate interpretation'. And in the public province, notions of individualism and novelty will sit at the very forefront of horizons of expectation for determining the value of auteurist texts. Henry Jenkins (through Michel de Certeau) has noted that we are conditioned as schoolchildren to read for authorial meaning and to 'successfully understand what the author was trying to say' (Jenkins 1992: 24). Given such a collective state of affairs, Jauss's hypothesis seems more instructive for the goals of this book when he writes (1982: 23) that 'the question of the subjectivity of the interpretation and of the taste of different readers or levels of readers can be asked meaningfully only when one has first clarified which transsubjective horizon of understanding conditions the influence of the text'.

At the root of the aesthetic judgement lies what de Man called 'the enigma of the relationship between the aesthetic and the poetic' (Jauss 1982: xxv) which, in the filmic realm, is transferred in the fluctuating altercation between the auteur picture and the genre picture. In Jauss's terms, an encounter with a new work will bring into play 'the horizons of expectation and rules familiar from earlier texts, which are then varied, corrected, altered or even just reproduced'. And, as Jauss reminded us 'variations and correction determine the scope, whereas alteration and reproduction determine the borders of the genre-structure' (1982: 23). The author helps the reader account for the former, of course, but in conducting an authorial case study we need to consider two overlapping horizons of expectation. The first will be the horizon of expectation for a film by David Lynch; the second is the more general horizon of expectation for the genre/auteur picture. It is only in the perception of the manner in how these horizons are met that the final judgement is brought about and the degree of the influence of a given text can be gauged. It is, then, to the construction of Lynch as a marketable author that we turn our attention to begin with.

CHAPTER 2

David Lynch: The Making of a Post-classical Auteur

That Lynch (or, for that matter, any other post-classical auteur) might be considered a 'free agent', operating independently of the system, can only ever be hypothetical. The proposition that authorship is manufactured by industry (rather than innate) is hardly new, but it is, all the same, an important point to clarify from the outset of our study. The principle, indeed, that the system and its films are malleable structures, adaptable to the tastes of different audience demographics, offers us the contextual framework we require for a more flexible understanding of the authored text to emerge. In verifying this point, this chapter, routed initially through the work of Staiger (2000) and Hoberman (1991), traces post-classical American art cinema, vis-à-vis Lynch's biographical legend, back to the American underground movement that flourished during the early-to-mid 1960s. We will begin by establishing, thus, how Lynch found his auteurist niche *within*, rather than outside, the post-classical system.

In the decade from 1976 to 1986 Lynch directed four feature films, his debut *Eraserhead*, *The Elephant Man* (1980), *Dune* (1984) and *Blue Velvet*. A concentration on this period allows us to put in place the contextual foundations for this book since it will help us trace Lynch's career path from comparative authorial anonymity to the full-blown status of auteur and deliver us, thus, to a point at which a horizon of expectation for 'A Film by David Lynch' was established. I will concentrate most of my discussion on two of these films – *Eraserhead* and *Blue Velvet* – since *The Elephant Man* and

Dune were, at the time of their release, neither promoted nor read as auteur films. A focus upon this period also provides a contextual framework for Lynch as a key figure in the maturity of post-classical American art cinema and will show the manner in which his legend was established through a confluence of promotion, publicity and criticism.

This chapter will also point to the capricious nature of the post-classical system, which adapts according to the demands of a dispersed modern audience demographic. Through the commentaries of Staiger and Hoberman, moreover, I will offer a focused historical illustration of how the Hollywood system has adapted to accommodate elements of modernist and avant-garde cinemas (a locus in which Lynch is situated) that duly set the ground for a more expressive new Hollywood to emerge. At the same time, this chapter will point us towards some of the broader themes of the book, such as how certain authorial assumptions fortify value judgements made upon cinematic artworks.

A signifying feature of an artwork is that it is personal; that the text somehow represents the personality of its author. Indeed, a studied or imagined account of an author's biography is the defining feature of the author function since, as Michel Foucault observed, the perception of an author's signature enables the spectator to 'explain the presence of certain events within a text, as well as their transformations, distortions and various modifications' (Foucault 1981: 143). It follows, then, that if we are to understand the reception and influence of a particular author's body of work, we are obliged, at the outset, to establish what horizons of expectation for that author's films are put into circulation through the sources that comprise their biographical legend.

Lynch's legend is built upon a juxtaposition: a childlike and personable Pacific North-Western conventionalism coupled with an interest in themes of a psychosexual and surreal nature. In his biography *Weirdsville USA, The Obsessive Universe of David Lynch*, Paul A. Woods titles his opening chapter 'All-American Martian boy' and proceeds by describing Lynch's idyllic suburban upbringing thus: 'raised in a pastoral version of the American dream [Lynch's] earliest memories are of long sunny days; bright flowers and neatly tendered lawns; early morning birdsongs and family visits; gifts from grandparents and good-natured sibling games; family camping vacations and winning Eagle Scout badges' (Woods 2000: 7). This setting has become one of the key signifiers in the reception of some of Lynch's most revered works: *Blue Velvet*, and the television series *Twin Peaks* (1990–91), its movie prequel *Twin Peaks: Fire Walk with Me* (1992) and *The Straight Story* (1999). At the same time, the impetus for the more disquieting elements of Lynch's films are here traced back to traumatic childhood events, including visits to his grandparents' home in Brooklyn. Woods offers the following quote from Lynch:

> In a large city I realized there was a large amount of fear. Coming from the Northwest it kind of hits you like a train. Like a subway. In fact, going into the subway, I felt like I was really going down into hell. As I went down the steps – going deeper and deeper into it – I realized it was almost as difficult to go back up and get out than to go through with the ride. It was the total fear of the unknown: the wind from those trains, the sounds, the smells, and the different lights and mood, that was really special in a traumatic way. (2000: 8)

Lynch's formal debt to surrealism, expressionism and other modernist art forms is also well documented and finds its roots in 1964 when, aged 18, Lynch took up full-time education in fine art at the Boston Museum School. A year later he headed for Europe where he planned to study painting in Salzburg. Having abandoned the trip after only 15 days, on the grounds that Salzburg was, as he put it 'so unpainterly and so *clean*', Lynch moved to Philadelphia where he studied at the Pennsylvania Academy of Fine Arts (PAFA). It was at PAFA that Lynch developed an interest in 'painting that moved' and he began to experiment with a 16mm camera. His first film, *Six Men Getting Sick* (1967) shared first prize at PAFA's end-of-year-show. Lynch's next short, *The Alphabet* (1968), helped him secure a $7,000 grant from the American Film Institute (AFI). But of most importance to Lynch was the fact that the AFI grants programme offered concrete distribution channels for its subsidised projects to be commercially exhibited.[1]

Completed in 1970, *The Grandmother* tells the story of a beaten and neglected boy who, imprisoned in a vast house, plants a seed from which a comely elderly woman emerges to befriend him. With *The Grandmother* Lynch showed modest regard for the tenets of verisimilitude. But the film (34 minutes long) marked a shift from Lynch's earlier experimental work towards a greater emphasis on live action tied with elements of a loose but tangible narrative development. This point is not without significance since it is an early indicator for Lynch's approval by the Hollywood system. Indeed, after he had completed *The Grandmother*, the AFI invited Lynch to study at its Centre for Advanced Film Studies in Los Angeles where he began work on his first feature, *Eraserhead*.

The production period for *Eraserhead* is enshrined in Lynchian legend. Some five years in the making, the film was funded partly by AFI grants and partly through other concessions, including a tight coterie of committed crewmembers working on percentage profits rather than salaries. Through Lynch's biographies, *Eraserhead* is presented as a truly independent labour of love and Lynch is duly cast – and casts himself indeed – as an artist dogmatically pursuing his creative vision. Fond references are commonly made, for instance, to an impoverished Lynch using the set for *Eraserhead* as a squat (the film was shot on location at abandoned buildings owned by the AFI) and his diverse sources of meagre income, which came in the shape of loans from his parents, money earned from shed building and wages from a job delivering the *Wall Street Journal*.[2]

Completed in 1975, *Eraserhead* secured its first theatrical release a year later, having drawn positive notices at the Los Angeles Film Festival. Ben Barenholtz, an exhibitor turned distributor of midnight movies, who had achieved a certain notoriety by having distributed Alejandro Jodorowsky's *El Topo* (1971), picked up the film and eventually secured regular screenings

Eraserhead: 'A dream of dark and troubling things'.

for it on the midnight circuit in 17 US cities. Lynch recalls how in LA, *Eraserhead* played for four years at the Nuart theatre: 'It only played one night a week, but every day of the week it was on the marquee. So whether people had seen it or not it became known' (Rodley 1997: 84). It was in LA, indeed, that *Eraserhead* came to the attention of Stuart Cornfeld and Mel Brooks who, as the film's executive producer and producer, respectively, were to hire Lynch as director for *The Elephant Man*.

Before we come to *The Elephant Man*, we might take time to consider *Eraserhead* within the legacy of the American underground movement. This is an important connection to establish since the underground cinema scene, which stretched from the late 1950s to the latter years of the 1960s, forthrightly declared its independence from Hollywood. In tracing a lineage from *Eraserhead* back to the underground scene, we can demonstrate that Bazin's famous declaration (made in 1957) that quality Hollywood films should be admired not only for 'the talent of this or that filmmaker', but also for 'the genius of the system' (Bazin 1981: 45), would appear to be a shrewd appraisal of how the system adapted to involve the auteur in its production and promotional arrangements.

Under a post-classical system it is commonplace for film directors to switch between production contexts. There are other industrial overlaps too and I will come to these in a later chapter, but assumptions about underground and independent, blockbuster and mainstream cinemas, and so on – as modes of production above, but not to the exclusion of, patterns of distribution and exhibition (since these will also shape horizonal expectations) – often pre-empt judgements made on those films under discussion. While it is not the case that these categories alone define the aesthetic ruling made upon a given text, as a rule of thumb, the issue of agency is central to how these judgements are reached. Artistic autonomy must be seen to exist, or, better still, prevail, in the former categories while it is nullified by economic imperatives in the latter. In other words, art cinema and commerce, despite being co-dependents, are still widely held to be inimical in most auteurist judgements.

With the exception of the failed blockbuster *Dune* – which Lynch disowned on grounds that his creative independence was over-compromised – and his bigger, more collaborative television projects, Lynch has gained artistic sovereignty over his films. He is determined upon the right to final cut, which so far as the artist and the auteurist are concerned, remains the ultimate proof of independence. The case for Lynch as an independent filmmaker is further strengthened in that he usually calls the shots in all three phases (pre-production, production and post-production) of the production process. The predicament with critical assessments founded on this principle alone is that they fail to take proper account (if they take account at all) of industrial imperatives that underpin those opinions. In other words, by focusing criticism upon the text to the exclusion of a given film's production, marketing, distribution and exhibition patterns, the critic separates the auteurist text from its historical and industrial contexts when these domains would do better to converge, to borrow a term used by Staiger (1992: 7), in a 'multiaccentual' writing of film history. This is not to say that we discount the author because of the vagaries of partisanship, but if the text is to feature in a materialistic history then we need to be clear from the outset that American auteurist cinema is what it is, a part of the system rather than something independent of it.[3]

Eraserhead and the New American Cinema

Eraserhead offers us a starting point from which we can trace Lynch's path through four production contexts: underground/midnight movie, Victorian period drama, science fiction event picture and American independent; the last being the point at which 'A Film by David Lynch' becomes a sub-genre in its own right. However, underground cinema, a term that originates from legitimate modes of independent production, distribution and exhibition, is associated with avant-garde films that were produced, or appropriated, in the name of a 'New American Cinema'. The underground movement, then, is allied initially with a scene of outspoken political opposition to Hollywood.

In keeping with the spirit of earlier modernist avant-gardes, the New American Cinema was borne of a policy. Referring to their manifesto in her essay 'Finding community in the early 1960s, Underground Cinema and sexual politics', Staiger cites Patricia Mellancamp and her summary of 'The First Statement of the New American Cinema Group':

> The initial impetus was to create alternative narrative features expressive of personal style and link up with the tradition of European art cinema and its U.S. exhibition circuit. The New American Cinema Group's statement of principles noted the development of a 'movement […] reaching significant

proportions.' It rejected censorship and called for new forms of financing, labor arrangements, distribution, and exhibition and for forms of appreciation for low-budget films from artists. [...] 'we are not joining together to make money. We are joining together to make films [...] we have had enough of the Big Lie in life and in the arts ... We don't want false, polished, slick films – we prefer them rough, unpolished but alive; we don't want rosy films – we want them the color of blood'. (Staiger 2000: 131)

Staiger considers the underground scene of the early 1960s under three headings: the tacit gay sexual liberation activities that critiqued heterosexual, same-race sexual norms; the expression of community in attending these films after midnight; and the ironic stylistic appropriations of popular culture that both opposed bourgeois culture and asserted 'rhetorical strategies for creating [...] subcultural community connections' (2000: 125–26). What we will see with *Eraserhead* is that while often referred to as an underground or midnight movie, it was a long way removed from the political impetus of the New American Cinema. Formally, too, *Eraserhead* nodded towards an earlier filmic avant-garde.

Staiger traces the underground's formal influences back to the teen-film market of the 1950s; the live, off-off-Broadway, New York theatre scene (a non-profit making public theatre that intermingled audience and performance and which was performed in interior public places such as cafes and churches) and in the literary field of 'beat' culture where, by Catharine R. Simpson's account (quoted by Staiger), writers such as Ginsberg, Duncan and Spicer 'appreciated alternative sexualities', through the idea of the 'rebel who seizes freedom and proclaims the legitimacy of individual desire' (though not, as was the predisposition within the underground film community, in terms of 'concealment and camp, parody and irony') (2000: 129–30). Drawing on a number of confrontational examples,[4] Staiger points to the fact that the critical reception of the films was uneven. The subject matter was one thing, but the production values of underground films were, depending on one's point of view, at best subversive, at worst pitiful. As Staiger says:

out-of-focus and overexposed images, lack of establishing shots and panning too fast [...] prevents the viewer's seeing what is likely (or hopefully) there. These were obviously studied effects by underground filmmakers [but] it is also clear that many people missed or resisted the jokes in the films because other things stood in the way. (2000: 139)

Staiger placed the geographical locations of the underground scene primarily in New York, with additional examples in Los Angeles and San Francisco. In its wider social contexts the underground referred also to 'the association of minorities not just in resistance against the dominant but also in a common cause unified by a political agenda for change' which, amongst New Yorkers at least, mustered connotations 'not of the hidden, but of alternative communities and political activism'. As a cinematic movement meanwhile, Staiger traces the community associations that characterised the underground's existence, back to the postwar films of Maya Deren, Amos Vogel and Jonas Mekas, who had between them created co-ops – films, distribution organisations, venues and journals – given over to non-traditional and avant-garde filmmaking (Staiger 2000: 135). We can say of *Eraserhead* that, while often written about as a personal labour of love and so lacking the same sort of community associations described above, the film sat closer in spirit to the films of Deren, Vogel and Mekas in its borrowings from pre-war European film movements, than to the spontaneous, playful attitude of the New American Cinema group. In this respect *Eraserhead* has been lauded for its technical assurance. Sean French, for instance, recognised a film lacking in 'the whole range of flaws that are traditionally associated with and excused in student or "underground" films' (1987: 101) including 'poor lighting, echoing sound, clumsy acting, rickety sets [and] shaky camerawork'. French, indeed, went so far as to describe the film as 'one of the major technical achievements of the decade' and even spoke of 'a one-man, shoestring nightmare version of *Citizen Kane* because of the vitality with which [Lynch] used every [formal] element available' (1987: 101).

The underground's association with teen-pix is a little less forthcoming. But as Staiger points out, not only were sexual themes and problems explicit in exploitation films – particularly horror (as indeed they are in *Eraserhead*) – the exhibition of teen-pix usually took place in neighbourhood theatres or at drive-ins; away from adults and where these exhibitions offered discrete sites for 'group exchange'.[5] Underground screenings offered a similar experience for adults through the late-night exhibition of underground films in independent and neighbourhood theatres. As Staiger notes (2000: 127) 'these screenings were much like the teen-pix of the era but with a [Greenwich] Village beat cast: audiences smoked marijuana and very vocally responded to the films'. It was by Staiger's account, though, that Andy Warhol's move into filmmaking in the mid-1960s marked the point at which the underground moved towards the 'aboveground' and underground films started their transformation into midnight movies.

The first Warhol 'serial', *Kiss*, was exhibited at New York's Gramercy Arts Theatre in the autumn of 1963. *Kiss* was originally (it was later cut and exhibited as a whole) shown as a series of 14,100-foot (three minute) silent reels that featured, as Hoberman (1991: 181–82) so candidly put it, 'pairings (both hetero and homosexual) passionately, dreamily, solemnly or campily chewing on each others faces'. However, it was the films made between 1964 and 1966 – including *Blow Job*, *My Hustler* and *The Chelsea Girls* – that drew national acclaim and which, as Staiger observed, worked to diminish the threat that non-traditional sexuality might have posed to middle-class communities. As she said 'when even *Newsweek* and *Life* could report on this cinema in a somewhat enthusiastic way, a sexual liberation seemed tolerable, maybe even fashionable' (Staiger 2000: 114). In Hollywood, meanwhile, the industry had reached a point of historical crossover where studio-financed films began to absorb the sensational elements that had distinguished the independents; a trend that, not by accident, coincided with the relaxation of the Production Code and liberal Supreme Court rulings on censorship.

The midnight scene continued to thrive into the early 1970s but if the midnight movies carried any opposition to Hollywood then the dissent had become increasingly opaque. Hoberman who, in his article 'Fear and trembling at the Whitney Biennial' (1991), delivered a heartfelt lament to the malaise in the American avant-garde cinema, did not miss this point, where once applied to the 'grandiose New American Cinema of the exciting underground' it had stirred connotations 'of a revolutionary elite, of subverting the status quo and advancing into some radiant future'; it now defined 'movies that are less in advance of than simply *other* than the commercial cinema'.[6] Indeed, by 1972 Hoberman saw the avant-garde entrench 'behind academic bulwarks', and become 'as concerned with the production of theory as with the production of films'. By Hoberman's reckoning, the upshot of this was that, while 'tolerated by universities and regulated by grants', the avant-garde had lost its culture of communal opposition, giving way instead to a film style that 'appeared to illustrate particular doctrines or appeal to specific audiences' which in turn gave rise to an 'institution subsidized mediocrity'. In Hoberman's assessment (1991: 176–77), the avant-garde's demise (or, given one's point of view, its transformation) was brought about by the emergence of the new Hollywood, since 'all the major filmmakers and a host of minor ones had come in from the cold to spawn a new generation of university trained filmmakers' (the movie brats in other words).

Hoberman did not, then, suggest that the avant-garde had reached its apotheosis in Hollywood. As he said 'just as the militant counterculture of the '60s had little impact on the American political system, so the underground failed to transform the economy of American movie consumption', while adding that 'if anything, Hollywood movies are more grossly formulaic than they were 15 years back – and their audiences no less passive' (Hoberman 1991: 177). All the same, the 'Greenberg-style modernism' which called attention to 'its own materials and axioms'[7] had become a perceptible feature of certain Hollywood films. Yet, in accounting for the underground's demise, it was the loss of a community of opposition over the blurring of aesthetic and industrial boundaries that Hoberman mourned most.

I will reconnect with *Eraserhead* in a moment, but on the last point Hoberman was to make specific reference to *Blue Velvet*. In conversation with John Hanhardt, the film curator at the Whitney, Hoberman wondered about the avant-garde credentials of *Blue Velvet*, given that the biennial featured five narrative feature films. Hanhardt was of the view that *Blue Velvet* was a commercial release whereas he felt an 'obligation to support work which is not enjoying marketplace support'. Presented with this rationale, Hoberman surmised that, defined only by what it was not (commercially supported), the avant-garde had been transformed into little more than a mode of exhibition (1991: 177). But even if aesthetic and exhibition boundaries had overlapped, and while exhibition strategies that allowed for communal political and cultural opposition had diluted, the midnight movie continued to flourish in neighbourhood theatres and in campus film societies. However, as Thompson and Bordwell (2003: 289) stressed in their account of structural and experimental film, the 'more commercially marketable elements of underground cinema obliterated its more experimental elements [and] by the mid-1970s, the underground film had become a marketable genre. It became the *midnight movie* or the cult film [that] provided [Paul] Morrissey, [John] Waters, [Pedro] Almodóvar and other directors an entry to commercial features'. It is in the exhibition context of midnight movies that we now come back to *Eraserhead*.

Eraserhead: A Midnight Hit

In their book *Midnight Movies*, Hoberman and co-author Jonathan Rosenbaum (1983: 214) proclaimed *Eraserhead* 'the most original and audacious film ever to become a midnight blockbuster…an almost miraculous achievement: an avant-garde hit'. However, Hoberman's sentiments appear less adulatory in his first, middling, review, There, he offered only grudging praise for a film that would constitute a 'revolutionary act if someone dropped a reel in *Star Wars*', but was 'too out looking for a cult' (Hoberman 1977). We may ask: what did Hoberman mean by this? And how does *Eraserhead* connect Lynch with contemporary Hollywood cinema?

Looking first at *Eraserhead* as a text, there was consensus that the film leaned heavily on the traditions of European art cinemas, notably surrealism and expressionism. The film's press book, circulated in conjunction with *Eraserhead*'s screening at the 1978 London Film Festival, now takes on historical significance since it offered a first introduction to the new American auteur, David Lynch. The film, bannered 'A dream of dark and troubling things', was introduced thus:

> This first feature by young American director, David Lynch, defies explanation and categorisation. 'Eraserhead' explores the dark areas where the spirit struggles with matter, where the subconscious is made manifest, where an inhuman environment is contrasted by the deepest human emotions. David Lynch incorporates the elements of science fiction and nightmare in a puzzling film of extraordinary power. 'ERASERHEAD' will establish Mr. Lynch as a master technician and visionary. (*Eraserhead UK Press Book* 1978) (copy held at the National Film and Television Archive, London)

In the trade press *Eraserhead* was reported as a commercial non-starter that *Variety* dismissed as a 'nonsensical [and] sickening bad-taste exercise', which featured, in Henry Spencer's (Jack Nance) murder of his sick and mutant child 'one of the most repugnant scenes in film history' (Mack 1977). Though clearly not to everyone's taste, wider critical notices did acknowledge *Eraserhead* as a film of considerable originality and technical aplomb. For Nigel Andrews the film had 'provoked varying degrees of shock, delight, nausea and giddy incomprehension', while the presence of the mutant infant 'swathed in mummy-like bandages', tilted 'the film towards macabre genius' (Andrews 1979), Paul Taylor (1979) described the film as an 'absurdist, surrealist treat of repulsive beauty and grisly comedy', while in his review for the film's British television premier in 1985, Gilbert Adair (1985) wrote that if 'an artefact so *sui generis* can be compared to anything on earth, it might be to the ghoulish party game in which the index finger of a blindfolded victim is steered into a soft, over-ripe tomato while one of his tormentors shrieks, "My eye! Oh God, what's happened to my eye!"'.

Writing in *Film Quarterly* nearly a decade after its initial release, K. George Godwin (1985: 37–43) was moved to ask why *Eraserhead* had become 'one of the most persistent and successful cult films of the midnight and art house circuits'. He brings to light two reasons that help us account for Lynch's move into the system proper as director of *The Elephant Man*.

In the first place, Godwin acknowledges that *Eraserhead* shared characteristics with the cult and midnight scenes citing its exhibition on midnight circuits and its 'shocking, even perverse images'. He contends, however, that *Eraserhead* differed from the cult/midnight class in two important ways. Firstly, with regard to the community experience that carried on at midnight showings in the wake of the underground's shift to aboveground, while other midnight successes – such as *El Topo* (with its 'relentless grotesquerie'), *The Rocky Horror Picture Show* (its 'innocent decadence') and the 'outrageous John Waters's entertainments' – shared with their audience the 'knowledge and rituals' that brought them together in 'communal experience', *Eraserhead* 'seemed in-turned' and 'obsessively introspective'. By means of its 'auditory and visual assault', which offered seemingly 'banal', 'meaningless' and 'inconclusive scenes', which in turn rendered the familiar 'frighteningly strange', Godwin suggests that the film offered an experience that was 'intensely personal, unshared'.

The second point emerges from the idea we have already touched upon, that *Eraserhead* was 'shot in beautifully atmospheric black-and-white, enhanced with a remarkably intricate, expressionistic soundtrack', that, for Godwin (1985: 37–43), represented 'artistry and technical skill' that was 'unique in low budget filmmaking'.

In *High Concepts*, Justin Wyatt (1996) reinforced the belief that *Eraserhead* was 'extreme and uncompromising'. But both Godwin and Wyatt recognised that the film was not, despite Mel Brooks's often quoted declaration to the contrary, the work of a 'raving madman' (Rodley 1997: 93). Indeed, Wyatt presents the argument that experimental filmmakers (including the likes of Mekas and Yvonne Rainer) whose work emphasises the structure and processes of filmmaking over narrative and linearity are not likely to appeal to the industry since they offer little potential for profit. Lynch, though, offered a more 'feasible case for assimilation', since for all its 'unbalanced composition and attraction to darkness', *Eraserhead* still 'exhibited strong ties to narrative' (Wyatt 1996: 90). Given this rationale, we could reasonably enough go a step further by speculating that Cornfeld, in his capacity as Executive Producer for *The Elephant Man*, would have recognised in *Eraserhead* a personal yet technically accomplished film. *Eraserhead* amounted then, to a crafted feature (produced, we will recall, over a period of five years) rather than a film that was spontaneous and polemical. This is perhaps what Hoberman was referring to when he described *Eraserhead* as 'too out looking for a cult', since the film demonstrated structured innovation through a technical fetishism that went against the unbridled reflexivity he mourned.

From Margin to Centre

In Lynch's journey from underground to aboveground we find more to strengthen this line of inference in his role as co-writer/director of *The Elephant Man*. At the time of its initial release *The Elephant Man* was not marketed or read particularly as a Lynch film. Lynch's agency was nullified rather than assimilated, since it deferred to the storytelling process. This point is illustrated in *The Elephant Man*'s promotional billing as a warmly humane true story. The banner aspect of the UK lobby poster quotes the film in John (the Elephant Man) Merrick's exasperated lament: 'I Am Not An Animal! I Am A Human Being! I ... Am ... A Man!' and underscores this with the declaration: 'The Elephant Man, an incredible but true story... probably the year's best film'. In the film's UK press book, attention was focused upon the story, 'as Lynch rightly remarks: "everything happened so easily, it's a real story in itself"', and towards the eminent cast list: Anthony Hopkins, Anne Bancroft and John Hurt. Other creative honours are directed not towards Lynch but to the film's cinematographer, Freddie Francis, who is represented as 'the acknowledged master of black and white photography', who used monochrome not for expressionistic effect but 'so as not to stress the horrific deformity of the Elephant Man [and] also to better capture the [Victorian] period'.[8]

The Elephant Man promotional poster.

Those critics who did hunt textual consistencies between *The Elephant Man* and *Eraserhead* only confirmed Lynch's creative anonymity. In his review, Henry Baker (1981) remarked that 'there is no civil war going on between form and content because Lynch, Freddie Francis, sound engineer Alan Splet, and the actors all contribute to the feeling of compassion and sadness that are the mainstays of the film'. Richard Combs (1980) opined that 'save for inspired opening and closing sequences there would have been little difference if the project had gone to Stanley Kramer', while Derek Elley (1981) was taken aback by the film's 'abundant good taste', when one might have expected 'Lynch to make a meal of The Elephant Man's more bizarre aspects'. In his review, John Pym even implied that Lynch had succumbed to the system in an act of artistic kow-tow. He drew an elaborate analogy between John Merrick's plight and Lynch's 'leap from *Eraserhead*... squarely into the lap of an "industry" production company', and argued that Lynch, like Merrick (who journeyed from freakish circus side-show exhibit to acceptance within Victorian middle-class society) 'reveals himself not so much as a wild child... as a *tabula rasa* [who] rapidly assumes the manners of the society he can only join by proxy' (Pym 1980/81).

Lynch has always insisted that *Dune* was the only finished film on which his agency was compromised. And, to reiterate, *Dune* was the one film on which he surrendered his right to final cut. I devote a later chapter to a discussion of Lynch's complicated authorship on *Dune*. At this point, suffice it to say that despite the fact that *The Elephant Man* was recognised by the Academy (the film received a total of eight Academy nominations including one for best director, although in the event it won none), on its initial cycle of release *Dune* was promoted and, on the whole, received as a science fiction event picture rather than a Lynch movie. All the same, despite its commercial and critical failure, out of his association with *Dune's* producer's – Dino and Rafaella De Laurentiis – Lynch found his industrial niche and was at last assimilated into the system, where he earned the rank of true auteur.

One need only look towards the two films Lynch made for the production company DEG (De Laurentiis Entertainment Group), to see the mutable nature of the system. *Dune* was an event movie with a budget in the region of $52m while *Blue Velvet* was a personal film produced at around one tenth its predecessor's cost (Hughes 2002: 68–73). Critics initially looked on *Dune* as a studio picture that was shaped aesthetically by the commercial interests of the film's financiers (Universal Pictures). *Blue Velvet*, on the other hand, is regarded as a personal work through which Lynch was allowed to express himself as he saw fit. Largely for this reason, *Blue Velvet* is able to compete as Lynch's masterpiece while *Dune*, for all its remarkable visual texture, is regarded as the turkey in his canon.

Selling *Blue Velvet*

I want to move towards the conclusion of this chapter by touching on the concept of postmodernism, the reason being that *Blue Velvet* is habitually read as typical of postmodern cinema. Indeed, the idea of *Blue Velvet* as a postmodern text will take up part of Chapter 4 devoted to the academic reception of the film. As an industrial structure, though, postmodern cinema applies to the middle ground that has emerged from the perceived divisions that existed historically between classical and modern cinema; a collapsing, in simpler terms, of high and popular cultures. In terms of its economic history, then, a postmodern cinema emerges within the shift from the Fordist mass production that characterised the vertically integrated studio era, to the plural forms of production, distribution and exhibition that have come to typify new Hollywood's global conglomeration and its laterally integrated divisions.

As a paradigm of these methods, *Blue Velvet* was produced on a budget of $5m by DEG and distributed by Twentieth Century Fox. In literature that refers to the film's production history, the point is made that De Laurentiis would only grant Lynch creative autonomy if he agreed to halve both the film's initial budget and his own salary.[9] The fact that DEG granted Lynch such freedoms might be further accounted for in De Laurentiis's policy of pre-selling his films through European and international contacts. It was in European markets that *Blue Velvet* built such a reputation that the encouraging pre-sales prompted De Laurentiis to seek a wider audience for the film in the US. By Michael Atkinson's account, Paul D. Sammon, an executive at DEG Studio, spent over six months 'platforming' the film at dozens of festivals and conventions. It was, according to Atkinson (1997: 16), only after *Blue Velvet* established a reputation through positive word of mouth in the US that 'DEG as a whole finally took notice, opening the film wide and promoting it full steam'.

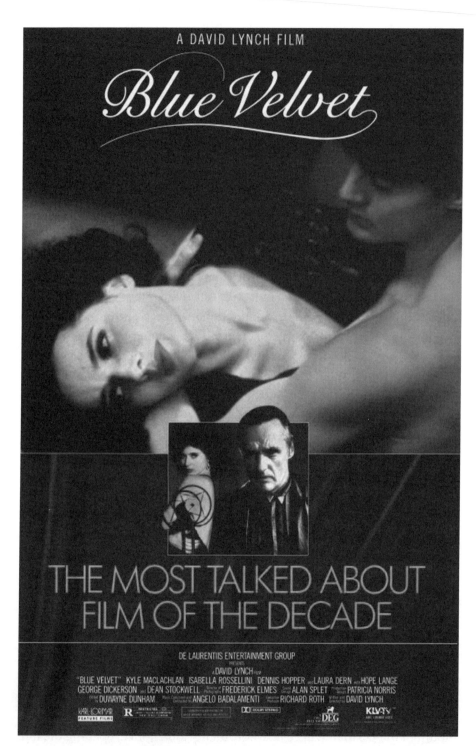

Blue Velvet promotional poster.

Firstly, then, *Blue Velvet* can be claimed as a postmodern film on the grounds that, as a modestly budgeted, personal movie, whose promotion and exhibition were more in tune with practices associated with regular studio pictures, it comprised a muddling of traditional marketing and exhibition domains for art films. Indeed, such blurring might be further evidenced through the film's trailer, which promoted the film on the promise of textual innovation and generic familiarity e.g. Jeffrey Beaumont (Kyle MacLachlan) spying through the slats of a closet; images of 'the Blue Lady', Dorothy Vallens (Isabella Rossellini), the alluring femme fatale figure; and the film's psychotic villain, Frank Booth (Dennis Hopper) shown in close shot in a fit of possessed laughter – all typical for a film noir-cum-mystery/thriller.

The trailer instructed audiences, meanwhile, that *Blue Velvet* came, 'from the mind of David Lynch', who had produced, 'a modern day masterpiece, so startling, so provocative, so mysterious, that it will open your eyes to a world you have never seen'. The trailer also flaunts positive critical notices, e.g. 'a sensual awakening of good and evil, a trip to the underworld' that was both 'a visionary story [and] a masterpiece' (David Thompson); 'it's erotically charged … one thing is for sure, you've never seen anything like it' (Peter Travers); 'a nightmarish, intensely disturbing exploration of the hidden side of the soul, it is sure to cause a sensation' (Ken Turan); and 'brilliant and unsettling … this is the work of an all-American visionary and a master film stylist' (Stephen Schiff).[10]

In its reception, critics found the film difficult to pin down since it disrupted a number of cultural presuppositions for commercial films. *Variety* thought that the film 'was a must for buffs and seekers of the latest hot thing', but predicted that 'mainstream viewers will likely find it unpleasant' (Cart 1986), while Betsy Berry (1988) referred to the film as a 'proclaimed cult film', as well as a 'significant addition to an already established genre: the detective story'. Hoberman (1991: 235) said he didn't know what to make of it but was sure that there hadn't 'been an American studio film so rich, so formally controlled [...] so charged with its maker's psychosexual energy since *Raging Bull*'. But if we are to proceed on the understanding that Lynch was (or is) a star auteur we should seek to establish how 'Lynch as personality' featured in the marketing and reception of *Blue Velvet* and, for the wider reach of this book, in subsequent texts carrying his name. This will help us ascertain what horizons of expectation were established for 'A David Lynch Film', with the release of *Blue Velvet*.

The utility of the auteur's name has become a much more routine feature in the marketing and reception of American films over recent years. Corrigan (1991: 103), for example, speaks of modern film authorship in terms of a 'commercial performance', in which certain auteurs benefit from a particular celebrity status. Corrigan explored this issue in his essay 'Auteurism and the new Hollywood' in which he refers to Quentin Tarantino's 1995 guest appearance on the American skit show *Saturday Night Live*.

Tarantino's performance featured a spoof TV talk show called 'Directors on Directing', which degenerates into a discussion on whether or not directors sleep with the actresses in their films. For Corrigan, this was evidence of 'un-abashed self-promotion', in which Tarantino's 'irreverently empty-headed' routine prompted Corrigan (1998: 39) to label him 'the quintessential 1990s' American auteur', who was 'fully bound up with the celebrity industry of Hollywood'. Although Lynch is rather less inclined towards barefaced acts of self-promotion, the link between him and Tarantino as 'commercial performers' is hardly an arbitrary one, since, with the release of *Blue Velvet*, Lynch's eccentric public persona was to feature prominently in the marketing and reception of his films. As Combs (1987) noted on *Blue Velvet*'s release, 'it is absurd, of course, to expect any author to "look like" his work, but the discrepancy between Lynch's apparent straightness, cleanliness and innocence, and the oozingly diseased world of his films must be so striking as to outrage the sense of the natural order of things'.

As Combs suggests, Lynch's ascendancy to status of star auteur was founded on a seemingly far-fetched correlation between author image and text that reached a high point in the early 1990s with the *Twin Peaks* television phenomenon.[11] Robert C. Cumbow (1978), when he concluded his review of *Eraserhead* by asking 'Who is this David Lynch?', was in search of an author who didn't yet exist. Cumbow was seeking a public figure that only properly emerged in the shape of publicity and self-promotion with the release of *Blue Velvet*. It is only at this point that Lynch gained the recognition as a film artist whose eccentricities could be sewn into the meanings of films carrying his name.

Writing on *Pulp Fiction*, David Thompson argued that Tarantino had superseded Lynch 'in the line of startling boy wonders'. While Tarantino (in keeping with his films' aesthetics) presented himself as an outspoken populist, dismissively defending claims of 'designer brutalism' with statements such as 'violence can be cool, it's just another colour to work with', and asserting that his brand of 'sophisticated storytelling and lurid subject matter [...] makes for an entertaining night at the movies' (Thompson 1994), Lynch came through as more introspective and adolescent-like, nonetheless driven by a dogged artistic plan.

The facets of Lynch's persona can be traced in a television programme he guest-presented for the BBC's respected arts programme, *Arena*, entitled 'Ruth, roses and revolvers: David Lynch presents the surrealists' (1987). In this programme, which was transmitted in the week of *Blue Velvet*'s UK release in April 1987, Lynch is given licence to discuss (without interruption from interviewers) excerpts from a series of his favourite experimental films and to infer their influence on his own ways of working. Specialist publicity such as this is planned to coincide with a film's release and in this case was geared towards establishing an auteurist standing for Lynch in advance of the viewers' encounter with *Blue Velvet*. This programme is all the more interesting since, to the best of my knowledge, it is the only recording where Lynch offers what amounts to something near a personal manifesto. In respect of Lynch's legend, then, it represents an attempt to establish his credentials among cultured cineastes – or even, the art lover per se – as a fine (cinematic) artist.

The programme (with editing credits given to Tim Cawston) is introduced with a brief montage of scenes from *Blue Velvet*, *Eraserhead* and *The Elephant Man*. Before a very cursory account of the latter two films (I am given to presume that *Dune* was omitted from this summary since as a sci-fi event picture, and a critically and commercially doomed one at that, it possessed the potential to confuse Lynch's figuring as an artist), an oration tells us that '*Blue Velvet* is the latest film by David Lynch. He's made some of the most original and disturbing films of recent years, films which create a world of their own where nothing is quite what it seems on the surface.' The link between Lynch and surrealist filmmaking is then made explicit with: 'Lynch goes back in time to the work of his kindred spirits of the past. He guides us through a rare collection of pioneering films made by some of the most influential artists of the 20th century: The Surrealists.' We are then introduced to Lynch who sets out his worldview thus:

The films you are about to see are among some of the most unusual ever produced. Tonight you will see nine excerpts from films made by some of the greatest artists of this century, the surrealists. They discovered that cinema was the perfect medium for them because it allowed the subconscious to speak. If surrealism is the sub-conscious speaking then I think I identify with it and I am somewhat surrealistic. I think that films should have a surface story but underneath it there should be some things happening that are abstract. There are things that resonate in areas that words can't help you find out about and these are sub-conscious areas. These surrealists who made the early films were shooting in the dark; they were feeling their way. But they've left behind a sign on a door that said once this door is opened it will make a way for a brand new kind of film. I'm very happy to be a fellow traveller with any of these guys ... for sure. (*Arena* 1987)

Throughout the programme Lynch celebrates a range of stylistic devices. Of Man Ray's *cinépoème, Emak-Bakia* (1926), for instance, Lynch champions Man Ray's automatic cinema, which utilised the improvisational technique of throwing a '$5,000 camera ... way up in the air and photographed all these sheep'; in Hans Richter's 'very special film', *Vormittagsspuk* (1928), Lynch admired its ability to manipulate time through a 'series of unexplained images' that touched upon 'strange feelings of death [and] opposites', and which was driven by the relentless rhythm of its experimental soundtrack; while in reference to Max Ernst's 'beautiful' episode *Desire*, from the collaborative feature *Dreams that Money Can Buy* (1944–46), Lynch spoke of Ernst's 'tender', skill in blending absurd humour in a 'dream like film ... because humour could just rip you right out of the dream'.

Despite his attraction towards the irrational and the automatic, taken on its own Lynch's worldview at least offered a purpose for the nuanced shape of his films. Under these terms, Lynch cast himself as a serious artist who, by incorporating surrealistic devices into feature-length narratives, was seeking a 'way for a brand new kind of film'. Yet the peculiar contrast between the producer (Lynch) and the product (*Blue Velvet*) caused a frisson that wilfully influenced future and retrospective readings of his work.

Coming back once more to Combs's comments, we find that the adjectives 'clean', 'straight' and 'innocent' relate to Lynch's conservative appearance: tidy, well pressed trousers and jacket and plain white shirt (without a tie but buttoned to the collar); and his clean-cut, well-groomed features: clean shaven, and short combed hair with a tidy centre parting. In respect of his 'innocence', Lynch appears younger than his 41 years. On this point *Variety* picked up on the physical resemblance between Lynch and *Blue Velvet*'s teenage sleuth, Jeffrey Beaumont, suggesting that the film's manicured small-town veneer was 'Like Lynch and his virtual lookalike leading man, Kyle MacLachlan [:] utterly conventional, placid, comfortable and serene' (Cart 1986). In his personality, meanwhile, Lynch embodied innocence in a way that seemed almost childlike. For instance, having quoted André Breton, who said of Ernst's work that it was so beautiful it was like 'a chance encounter on a dissecting table of a sewing machine and a bicycle', Lynch opined, without any apparent irony or mischief 'so you can see it really is beautiful'. Likewise, in his discussion of Marcel Duchamp's 'Discs' (*Dreams that Money Can Buy*), and Duchamp's belief that the cinema had powers of hypnosis, Lynch said 'for sure the film has a tremendous power but I'm not so sure I believe in hypnotism', while concluding (closing an eye) 'I sorta watched this with one eye shut and dart over to see the rug [placed somewhere, presumably, between him and the screen] from time to time'.

Lynch's personality duly carried over into press interviews and reviews where he was sometimes likened to Jimmy Stewart. Pauline Kael (1986) wondered whether Lynch 'might turn out to be the first popular surrealist – a Frank Capra of Dream Logic', while an article carried in *Newsweek* suggested that Lynch had become 'famous for his Jimmy Stewart style', and added 'He loves vanilla milkshake and says things like "golly gee", which makes the darker side of his imagination all the more startling' (McGuigan 1986). Geoff Andrew, meanwhile, saw *Blue Velvet* as '"Eraserhead" made for the contemporary world', and suggested that 'anyone worth their cinematic salt knows this guy is *weird*'. Andrew (1987), though, approached the film with a measure of caution: 'see "Blue Velvet" of course, and wonder at the fertility of its vision. But don't be taken in by the persuasiveness of Lynch's bug-eyed look at humanity. Originality and genius, after all, are not everything; a little honesty, a little moral awareness is also worth bearing in mind'.

Corrigan (1991: 103) argued that auteurism defined 'almost exclusively as publicity and advertising' allows the reader to predict 'the meaning of the film in its totalising image that precedes the movie in the public images of its creator'. On the evidence presented here, Lynch would seem to exemplify these industrial developments. Indeed, under these terms, the Lynchian factor was now set and a horizon of expectation for 'A Film by

"BLUE VELVET"

DEG

DE LAURENTIIS ENTERTAINMENT GROUP

Writer/Director David Lynch ("Dune," "The Elephant Man," "Eraserhead") now brings to the screen "BLUE VELVET," a De Laurentiis Entertainment Group release.

Lynch publicity portrait for *Blue Velvet*.

David Lynch' had been established. The auteurist might now be able to predict, for example, proverbial but strange dream worlds in which themes of a psychosexual nature are played out. She or he might also begin to make new intertextual associations between creative associates such as Frederick Elmes (cinematography), Alan R. Splet (sound design), Angelo Badalamenti (score) and, of course, performers. Indeed, MacLachlan, in his role as the central protagonist across a number of Lynch's films was, as we will begin to see in the following chapter, often understood to function as Lynch's alter ego.

What, we might now ask, becomes of the text, if our analysis is extended through empirical accounts alone? Surely then we would lose sight of the 'personality of the text' that might instigate the search for an author to begin with? It is with these questions in mind that I want to turn my attention to contemporaneous and retrospective readings of *Dune* and to take account of the shifting horizonal paradigms that accounted for its classification as a novel adaptation, a science fiction event movie and 'A Film by David Lynch'. Given Lynch would rather be disassociated with the film, we may also start to ask how the author functions for pleasure in the hermeneutic act.

CHAPTER 3

Meanings and Authorships in *Dune*

This book is more or less chronologically organised according to the sequencing of Lynch's cinematic canon. My rationale for breaking this rule on *Dune* (and, for different reasons that I will come to in due course, *INLAND EMPIRE*) is that *Dune* did not, strictly speaking, become 'A Film by David Lynch' until after the release of *Blue Velvet* (in 1986). Even so, *Dune* still does not rank highly amongst Lynch's biographers chiefly because it was conceived of (and marketed initially) as an event movie (rather than a personal film), and because it was a filmed adaptation of a million-selling novel with its own author: Frank Herbert. Indeed, the conflict of interests on *Dune* – including the demands made on him to stay true to the essence of the source novel – prompted Lynch to all but disown the film, having described onerous production processes which he believed had all but annulled his agency.

But this information should not deter us from investigating *Dune* as a Lynch film; we should treat *Dune* and Lynch's authorial disclaimer rather as *an opportunity*, through which, we can begin to ask some questions of post-structural criticisms and the bordering concerns around authorship and textual pleasure that Barthes raised, firstly through the concept of the 'death of the author', and in his subsequent books *S/Z* and *The Pleasure of the Text* (both published towards the mid-1970s). Indeed, as we are about to address ourselves to the topic of poetics and authorial spheres of influence, it is appropriate that we should proceed by firstly reacquainting ourselves with Barthes's strategic principles.

In any thoroughgoing reception study of Lynch, we would find abundant evidence that his films divide opinion, so we must hesitate before assigning given effects to his films. Having said that, Barthes's attempts to account for the workings of texts outside a single structure opened up possibilities for accounting for structural differences between texts and, within those differences, distinctions between narrative effects and narrative pleasures could emerge. In Barthes's prototype, we can easily conceive that the classical realist text will act as a horizontal paradigm (although Barthes doesn't use this term of course) since it will solicit clear expectations about how a given story will be told. The established view demands that for a text to provide pleasure it must be presented in a manner that is perceived by the reader to be realistic. The classical realist narrative (according to Colin MacCabe, the transferral from the nineteenth-century realist novel into classical realist cinema comes via 'the narration of events through images' rather than in the written prose of the novelist)[1] demands, above all else, that temporal and spatial links between events in the narrative are logically linked. At the same time, the series of events that governs the development of the story will be organised around the clearly defined motivations and actions of individual characters, or heroes.

In *S/Z*, Barthes argued that the realist text is governed by an internal logic – what he called an 'intra-textual economy' – and under this rule every detail of action plays one or more functional roles within the unfolding of the narrative (although ideally this function should not be obvious to the reader). The classical narrative amounts, therefore, to *a system*; one that adheres to a highly crafted and selective process that produces enclosed, or 'readerly', texts. As Barthes (1975b: 156) put it, 'the readerly [text] is controlled by the principle of non-contradiction' and 'by multiplying solidarities, by stressing at every opportunity the compatible nature of circumstances [...] narrated events' give the impression of being held 'together with a kind of logical "paste"'. The other type of text – that is, the more ambiguous open-ended, or 'writerly', text – will create infinite possibilities for creating meaning. The writerly text, according to Barthes 'is ourselves writing, before the infinite play of the world (the world as function) is traversed, intersected, stopped, plasticised, by some singular system (ideology, genius, criticism) which reduces the plurality of entrances, the opening of networks, the infinity of languages' (1975b: 5). But taking in hand Barthes's call for the author's death, we come across a paradox because the type of text Barthes preferred, the writerly text (although it is prudent to note that actual texts fall somewhere within the scale of readerly and writerly boundaries), usually makes fervent demands of an author, who will be, in almost every case, construed through the institutionalised methods Barthes disliked: 'ideology, genius and criticism'.

It was in *The Pleasure of the Text* (1975a), that Barthes explained his well-known distinction between textual pleasures. The text of pleasure (*plaisir*) is one that 'grants euphoria [...] the text that comes from culture and does not break with it' and is linked thus to 'the comfortable practice of reading'. The text of bliss (*jouissance*), meanwhile 'imposes a state of loss, the text that discomforts (perhaps to the point of a certain boredom), unsettles the reader's psychological assumptions, the consistency of his tastes, values and memories [and] brings to a crisis his relation with language' (1975a: 14). The former effect is then associated with readerly texts, the latter with the writerly texts. Yet even though in *The Pleasure of the Text* he maintained that 'as institution, the author [was] dead', Barthes was ready to concede that she or he might offer pleasures in private; albeit that Barthes seemed to view the author as a seductive presence (who may compromise the reader). Barthes, in fact, discussed the text as a 'fetish object', and 'lost in the midst of a text', he argued 'there is always the other, the author' (1975a: 27).

We must wait until the latter stages of this chapter in order to have a body of empirical evidence to call upon when addressing ourselves more fully to the problems that arise through Barthes's ideas on reading pleasures and authors. But there is a further emerging attitude that we must approach before we can turn to the text itself. This is the view expressed by Barthes's compatriot and contemporary Foucault, who, through an analysis of the 'author function' (in his 1969 essay 'What is an author?'), spoke of the hermeneutic tasks performed by an author's biography. Foucault believed that an author's biography performs a 'classificatory function' and noted subsequently that scholarly convention dictated that we must 'ask of each poetic or fictional text: from where does it come, who wrote it, when, under what circumstances, or beginning with what design?'. Foucault remarked (1981: 141), indeed, that 'the meaning ascribed to [the text] and the status or value accorded it depend upon the manner in which we answer these questions'. The implicit criticism behind this statement is that we have been 'conditioned' to learn about literature in prescribed ways (when, certainly in Barthes's view, a revolution was what was called for). Under its biographical habituation, indeed, logic dictates that however much we might speculate on a text's meaning, a novel such as *Dune* will only reveal its true secrets once we learn about the story of Herbert's life and something of his opinions on life.

Barthes's and Foucault's descriptions appear critical of a conservative attitude towards reading that sees the author and their biographical profile as a means of providing an inflexible, methodical mode of decryption. But where we must surely be at variance with Barthes is in his assertion that the author's 'civil status [and] his biographical person have disappeared' and so 'no longer exercise over his work the formidable paternity whose account literary history, teaching, and public opinion had the responsibility of establishing and renewing' (Barthes 1975a: 27). It is patently not true to say that the author is dead, either as organisation or as custom. But Barthes's criticism remains valid in any case if we accept the fact that it mounts a challenge to the convention that dictates that meanings are confirmed or deduced in logical accordance with the known intentions of the author; that is, any argument that lends itself to the suggestion that the testament of the author – in cases where it is documented – should act as the *'formidable' last word* in the interpretative act.

It is undoubtedly true that there is a tendency amongst seekers of the truth to concede all precedence to the author's testament; to get to the essence of the text in this way. But what we are shown in the biographical accounts of Lynch's *Dune* is evidence of a writerly author function, especially given that Lynch's biographers are apt to write elements of *Dune* as an auteurist text, despite being fully aware of Lynch's efforts to distance himself from the finished film. Such writerly practices are not the special province of the professional biographer, of course, and the modern day auteurist is by no means necessarily of scholarly intentions; she or he need not be because the auteur is no longer the private property of an academic select. Indeed, the film author, as we have ascertained already, is these days a freely available figure invoked through public discourse. Livingston pointed us towards what seems a more accurate account of how the modern auteur functions for pleasure when he made the following observation in relation to real and imagined film authorships:

> For various practical reasons, most film spectators simply do not know what went on during the making of the film they are viewing, yet the interpretive process requires them to attribute attitudes and implicit

meanings to someone's expressive activity. It would be in many cases a factual error for such viewers to assume that the expressed attitudes were those of the text's maker(s), so it is best for them simply to make believe that the attitudes expressed are those of a fictional author. Such make-believe cannot be wrong, because it is just a fiction that enhances the viewer's appreciation of the film. (Livingston 1997: 146)

As convincing as Livingston's argument is, the demands of a textual historicity are such that we must not be tempted to demote modes of production to a peripheral role (because it is spectators who count most). If we were to choose to do so, then, like the unfettered auteurist Livingston pictures, we could only guess about the intentions of the text; our goals are more considered and we would stand to learn nothing of the precise historical significance of the encounters that emerge in correspondences between individual texts and audiences were we to do so.

As regards the idea of collaborative authorships, such concerns being of pertinence in more egalitarian authorial undertakings, we do not find anything to contradict what we have already learned. Because the reader chooses to divide into parts, and then allot, creative signs to more than one individual, does not mean that all humanist inadequacies are prevailed over. Berys Gaut is amongst those who advocate this 'more careful treatment' of film authorship, believing, indeed, that the reader stands to gain a 'more enriching understanding of films' via the route of collaborative authorship. Gaut (1997: 161–69), in fact, wondered: 'what might be gained by speculating on the psychology of a kind of super-intelligent octopus [the auteur], whose tentacles control the myriad machines of cinema and reach into the very souls of the actors?'. Conversely, it can be through special actors – *those actors who play the hero* – that the writerly inclined auteurist will stand to find the most convenient path back through the text to the soul of the true auteur.

Finding Authorial Narrations in *Dune*

Having already established the basis of Lynch's legend, our task now will be to explore the terms under which meanings have been generated in relation to *Dune*, directed by Lynch from his own adapted screenplay of Herbert's epic (and for many fans, sacrosanct) science fiction novel. As I have indicated above, *Dune* offers a rich case study for an auteur analysis since it is a film that has had to adapt to multiple authorships. From a Lynchian perspective, it is usually seen as his least personal work – an event movie no less – and as such it is perceived amongst his biographers as the most unsatisfying film in his canon. It is then the goal of this chapter to analyse *Dune*'s meanings in relation to biographical accounts founded on the tenets of early auteurism, such as those by Chion and Atkinson, and journalistic writings, including Hoberman's article 'The end of science fiction', first published in 1985 (1991: 206–10). As has already become clear, our task is not to dismiss auteurism as humanist idealism. Rather, the outcome of this chapter seeks to consider, through Barthes's writings once more, the thresholds of pleasure that the author might offer in the reception of the text.

In light of the late 1960s Franco-philosophical interventions of structuralism and post-structuralism, to which both Barthes and Foucault were key contributors, the idea of the author genius came to be viewed in terms of a mythical romanticism. Through Barthes's call for the death of the author, moreover, hermeneutic rights were to pass from producer to reader. As a consequence, a succession of revised auteurisms emerged over the years all of which wrestled with early auteurism's idealistic shortcomings. But the evolution of auteurism through more empirical territories should not obscure the fact that the textual fetishism associated with early auteurism remains the dominant public channel by which the poetic film has come to be enjoyed and understood. In fact, it is the aspiration of this chapter to take account of how the author functions for pleasure in the reception of a text that *is not*, in any accurate sense, auteurist in nature.

One of the reasons why *Dune* resonates as an authorship study is that it is an adaptation of a revered literary work, recognised and understood both as the gifted work of an author (Herbert) and as a formulaic literary adaptation. As a consequence *Dune* has proved the most troublesome text for biographers to take auteurist account of. Martha P. Nochimson summed up this feeling in her book *The Passion of David Lynch* (1997: 123) when she wrote that '*Dune* is the only Lynch film about which there is valid general agreement that it doesn't work'.

Like its predecessor, *The Elephant Man*, on its theatrical release *Dune* was not promoted, nor widely read, as 'A Film by David Lynch'. As I have stated already, his manifestation in the promotion and reception of his films only properly occurs through subsequent films. This fact points to the momentary and volatile nature of meanings, since in retrospective promotions and readings (that now tie in Lynch's name), the creative sources in *Dune* are often disputed and horizonal expectations potentially muddled. As an added complication to *Dune*'s hermeneutic changeability, there now exists different versions of the film: the theatrical version and an extended 'more coherent', version re-cut for domestic markets. And while the theatrical version came to appear on video formats as 'David Lynch's Stunning Sci-Fi Spectacular', the extended 'Special TV Edition' conceals Lynch's name on its sleeve altogether.[2] In the credits for the latter, indeed, Lynch's name as director and screenwriter is replaced by the pseudonyms Allen Smithee and Judas Booth respectively.[3]

Generally speaking, modernism honoured the status of the author under the proviso that she or he was engaged in the expressive pursuit of originality and truth. It was under the direction of structuralism and its focus on the structuring of language that the author came to be viewed as an ideologically constituted agent. The myth of artistic genius was rejected on the understanding that an individual could not traverse the borders of language. The artistic genius came to viewed thus as an edifice of market forces.

Barthes and Foucault were key influences in rethinking the author, and where she or he stood in relation to the interpretation of the texts. Foucault, as we have learned, saw authors as serving institutional interests through their classifying function, while Barthes (1977: 147) addressed himself more immediately to the act of reading and pleasure and proposed thus, that the authored text be understood as something other than 'a line of words releasing a single "theological" meaning (the "message" of the Author God)'. For Barthes, indeed, the text should be seen rather as a 'multi-dimensional space in which a variety of writings, none of them original, blend and clash' (1977: 147). In putting these ideas to the test, we will pursue the theme of the author function firstly in terms of how transcripts of authorial intention might operate in the act of interpreting Frank Herbert's *Dune*. Let us proceed, then, with a brief literary context for the extended *Dune* chronicles.

Between December 1963 and May 1965, the American science fiction magazine *Analog* published the first three episodes of the *Dune* saga. Following on from this, Herbert's expanded story was first published in the US as a novel in 1965. In his essay 'American science fiction since 1960', J.A. Sutherland (1979: 162) situates *Dune* and other 'million-seller' books, *Stranger in a Strange Land* (1961) and *2001: A Space Odyssey* (1968), within the context of a 'new mass-readership' for 'cult' science fiction. Indeed, such has been the *Dune* saga's fan base that up until his death in 1986, Herbert had published five sequels and pre-sequels.[4] In due course the novels prompted associated media and ephemera – including, of course, the filmed adaptation of the first novel in 1984.

Set in the year 10191, across four distant planets, *Dune*'s narrative is the tale of feuding monarchies contesting the control of a desert planet (Arrakis/Dune), which is the most important planet in the known universe since its sand produces a spice that is able to extend life, fold space and expand consciousness. In respect of its generic appearance, the novel is seen as something of a curious hybrid. In his book, *Science Fiction, the New Critical Idiom* Adam Roberts refers to *Dune*'s 'groundedness in a medieval literature and film', and its 'almost medieval technological non-sophistication'. Indeed, Roberts observed that there are:

> two areas in which *Dune* introduces items that we might think of as technological nova [that] are compromised by the logic of the novel. One is the interstellar travel, a necessary precondition for the book we might think; and yet this premise is explained not scientifically but mystically. [The second is a] fascination with the toy-like ingenuity of machine technology [that is] ultimately undercut by a deeper sense of satisfaction at a retro-defined sense of chivalric conflict. This happens on a personal level, so that the battles of *Dune* are fought by individuals with knives and swords. (Roberts 2000: 36)

For all its elements of mysticism, *Dune* is still highly regarded as a modernist text. In his essay 'Manifest destiny: science fiction and classical form', for instance, Joseph M. Lenz (1983: 47) suggested that *Dune*'s narrative was 'a modern classic' since it opens up 'a virtually infinite set of questions' and, as such, the reader 'cannot rely on [his or her] conventional expectations' for science fiction literature. *Dune*'s symbolism has been interpreted thus, according to Herbert's worldview and the author's stated affiliations with the 1960s American counterculture movement. In *Frank Herbert, The Maker of Dune, Insights of a Master of Science Fiction* (1987), Tim O'Reilly offers an expedient example of the manner in which *Dune*'s meanings have come to be regulated under the terms and conditions of Herbert's biography.

We learn from O'Reilly's book that Herbert conceived of *Dune* as a trilogy pertaining to the dangers of messianic followings. This theme can be discerned in the novel's figuring of its central protagonist, Paul Atreides (renamed Muad'Dib), whose arrival on Arrakis is hailed by the planet's indigenous nomads (Fremen) as the coming of the prophet ('the voice from the outer world' to use the novel's terminology). The Fremen believe that Paul will bring rain to the desert planet and will lead them in jihad against its colonisers who control Arrakis's spice mining. The fascistic theme is reinforced through Paul's selection by a mystic sisterhood, the Bene Gesserit. Paul's mother, Lady Jessica, had in fact been ordered to produce a daughter with Duke Leto Atreides II, but defied that order – 'for reasons she confesses have never been completely clear to her' – in conceiving a son. According to the novel, the Bene Gesserit programme has as its target the breeding of a person they labelled 'Kwisatz Haderach' a term the sisterhood used to signify 'one who can be many places at once'; a human figure with mental powers permitting him to understand and use higher order dimensions (Herbert 1998: 425).

Herbert expounded this dimension of the novel in terms of his anxieties over the consequences of power, politics and economics and their 'logical consequence, war'. In keeping with the general mood of the counter-culture group, Herbert believed that Western civilisation was in danger of becoming dependent on 'people [giving] over every decision-making capacity to any leader [John F. Kennedy, Adolph Hitler, George Patton] who can wrap himself in the myth fabric of society'. Herbert also reveals that events in *Dune*'s narrative were analogous with contemporary political and economic events: 'corruption and bribery in the highest places, whole police forces lost to organized crime [and] regulatory agencies taken over by the people they are supposed to regulate' while 'the scarce water of Dune [was intended as] an exact analog of oil scarcity. CHOAM [the name given by Herbert to a military force which governs the mining of the spice in *Dune*] is OPEC' (Herbert 1987: 97–98).

Authorial significance is also read into *Dune*'s planet topographies because Herbert (who in his previous career as a journalist had written several articles on the US Department of Agriculture's attempts to control coastal sand dunes) had made public his concerns with how humankind had 'inflicted itself upon the planet'. And finally, given the context of the 1960s counterculture, the hallucinogenic properties of the spice extracted from the sand on Arrakis became analogous with the widespread use of LSD since drugs (so Herbert believed) only 'enable people to endure an otherwise intolerable existence' and to suffer at the hands of 'the production/consumption treadmill' (Herbert 1987: 106). It is, however, through Herbert's mystical interests that *Dune* begins to invite composite readings. Herbert wrote:

> In studying sand dunes, you immediately get into not just Arabian mystique but the Navaho mystique and the mystique of the Kalahari primitives and all [...] I [found through research] fresh nuances, things in religions, in psychoanalytic theories, in linguistics, economics, philosophy, in theories of history, geology, anthropology, plant research, soil chemistry, in the metalanguages or pheromones. A new field of study rises out of this like a spirit rising from a witch's caldron: *the psychology of planetary societies* [...] Now we have stories with which we go on after we finish reading them. I deliberately did this with *Dune*. (1987: 106)

The topic of authorial sovereignty will occupy much of our subsequent discussion. What is key to underline in concluding our analysis of Herbert's book is that although *Dune* is often read as a modern work, this is not in any uncompromising structural sense. By way of contrast, Lynch is an author who regards himself, and is often regarded, as an artist not restricted by the limits of history and language (although as we saw in the previous chapter, he does not necessarily repudiate narrative).

Filming *Dune*

Given *Dune*'s healthy sales (and a ready-made potential to yield sequels) a filmed version of the book augured well as a money-spinning venture. Janine Pourroy and Don Shay chart *Dune*'s pre-production history in their detailed article 'The shape of Dune' (1985). In summary, they explain how in 1972 Arthur P. Jacobs's company APJAC – a production company that had scored commercial success in the 1960s and early 1970s with the *Planet of the Apes* cycle[5] – bought a nine-year option on the novel. However, following Jacobs's sudden death in 1973, the rights to the novel passed to the French businessman Michael Seydoux, who acquired the option on *Dune* for the Parisian based production company, Camera One.

It was at Camera One that a filmed version of *Dune* entered a protracted two-year period of pre-production. The project was abandoned once a third of the initial $6m budget had been spent and Seydoux had failed in his attempts to secure further financial backing, since director/screenwriter

Jodorowsky's elevated artistic ambitions did not augur well as a viable business option. Seydoux eventually sold the option on *Dune* to the Italian film mogul Dino De Laurentiis in 1976. Some three years later, another troubled period of pre-production commenced with Ridley Scott as director and Rudolph Wurlitzer as screenwriter. On this occasion, however, the film's backers, Universal Pictures, were unhappy with Wurlitzer's screenplay (since it placed emphasis on the novel's theme of political insurrection and explored the idea of an incestuous relationship between Paul and his mother) and the *Dune* project was shelved once more.

Following the collapse of the Scott/Wurlitzer project in 1981 De Laurentiis renegotiated Herbert's contract on the rights to *Dune* (though Herbert is not credited on *Dune* other than 'Based on the novel by Frank Herbert') and its sequels (written and unwritten). Pre-production commenced in earnest on the first filmed version of *Dune* in June 1981 when the film's producer, Rafaella De Laurentiis (daughter of Dino), secured the services of Lynch as director and screenwriter. We shall return to Lynch's current status as an auteur and the choice of him as director of *Dune* shortly, but at the time he was hired, Lynch, as we have established, was relatively inexperienced and not well known as a director.

Lynch had originally collaborated on a screenplay for *Dune* with Eric Bergen and Christopher de Vore (he had worked with both men on the script for *The Elephant Man*). However, according to Lynch, De Laurentiis had been unhappy with the direction of the writing since it deviated too much from the source novel. In the event, De Laurentiis allowed Lynch to take on screenplay credits for himself on the stipulation that he worked in consultation with Herbert. This resulted in a compromise of interests on which Lynch was drawn into the following discussion with Rodley:

> *Rodley*: The worlds of *Eraserhead* and *The Elephant Man* are small – sometimes microscopic. *Dune* – even in novel form – creates a big, potentially unwieldy universe of several worlds. How did you deal with that initially?
>
> *Lynch*: I had a lot of talks with the author, Frank Herbert, concentrating on every line in the book. There are so many things in it that seem to contradict themselves as you get into it. And there's many confusing things in it. Many strange bits of information, technology and mythology. And it's like – where's the story, you know? The more you get into it, the more it's hard to hold on to. But I was way down the line before I started having these feelings. I really went pretty insane on that picture. (Rodley 1997: 114–15)

In *Lynch on Lynch*, *Dune* is presented (as it is in all of Lynch's biographies) as the film that he finds least satisfying since he sees it as an endeavour in which his agency was breached. Lynch explains how, before agreeing to work on *Dune*, he had turned down an offer from George Lucas to direct *Return of the Jedi* (1984) because he 'never really liked science fiction', and that '*Star Wars* was totally George's thing'. His rationale for working on *Dune* was that he was drawn to the novel's textures: '*Dune* was different; it has believable characterizations and depth. In many ways, Herbert had created an *internal* adventure, one with a lot of emotional and physical textures' (Rodley 1997: 113–14).

The implication we draw from these statements is, of course, that Lynch felt that working on *Dune* (rather than *Return of the Jedi*) would allow him liberty to pursue his particular creative interests since he viewed *Dune* as an open-ended, or writerly, text. The implication, too, is that even under the creative constraints associated with working on an event movie – by Pourroy and Shay's account (1985), *Dune*'s financiers, Universal Pictures, had set a production budget of $50m and a further $26m for the film's marketing – Lynch felt he would still be able to retain an acceptable degree of creative autonomy.

Despite this initial optimism, however, Lynch proceeds to bemoan the creative constraints placed upon him by the film's producers and financial backers. These include the insistence that *Dune* be given a PG certificate thereby maximising the film's potential for box office returns (of which Lynch said,' You can think of some strange things to do but as soon as they throw in a PG, a lot of them go out of the window') and the imposition of a running time of two hours and 17 minutes. This point is particularly significant since not only did Lynch object to the spoiling of the filmed material in this way, but critical receptions of the film often cite a compacted narrative and a subsequent lack of narrative solidity as the film's basic flaw. But Lynch's more general disquiet with *Dune* is summed up in the following statement:

> I never carried anything far enough for it to be really my own. I had the feeling that Dino and Rafaella wanted something, and then there was Frank Herbert's book, and trying to be true to it. So you're really locked into a specific corral. And it's hard to break out of that. I didn't really feel I really had permission to make it my own. That was the downfall for me. It was a problem. *Dune* was like a kind of studio film. I didn't have final cut. And,

> little by little, I was subconsciously making compromises – knowing I couldn't go here and not wanting to go there. (Rodley 1997: 115–20)

Although by his own admission *Dune* is the least personal of his films, Lynch does discuss elements of the film on which he was able to impose his signature. These elements refer almost exclusively to the look of *Dune* (although he does suggest that the character of Paul is a typical Lynchian hero: 'the sleeper who must awaken and become what he must become') (Rodley 1997: 116). All the same, in our example doubt can be cast on the auteurist dogma that demands that a director will at least exert total control over a film's mise en scène. With reference to *Dune*'s set and costume design, for instance, Lynch speaks of wishing he had been able to go further with 'factories and rubber and some industry […], instead of long, flowing robes and that medieval sort of feel' (Rodley 1997: 116). And although it was mandated that *Dune* be shot in colour, Lynch had wanted to de-saturate the colour, against the wishes of *Dune*'s producers. The process of compromise is illustrated in an interview in the trade journal *American Cinematographer* with *Dune*'s cinematographer, Freddie Francis, who remarked that he'd 'gone very low in key for color, sometimes hardly as low as David [Lynch] would *like* to go, but one has to think of other people who have to sell the film' (Mandell 1984). In spite of auteurist discrepancies such as these, *Dune* was, nonetheless, promoted as a new departure for the science fiction event film.

Placing the Author in *Dune*

The choice of Lynch as director added to the commotion around *Dune*'s commercial and critical failure. Yet according to pre-publicity for the film, *Dune*'s producers had chosen to think of the film in terms of a new alternative for the genre. In discussion with Chris Auty at a lecture given at London's National Film Theatre coinciding with the film's UK release, Rafaella De Laurentiis articulated the production company's ambitions in the following terms:

> To do a special effect movie today is a question of money. I'm not saying everybody, but almost everybody can do special effects. And we did not want to do a hardware movie, there are too many out there. We wanted a stranger; different movie that would take you places. People said the $40m [sic] was not the gamble but David Lynch […] What makes *Dune* a great

picture? I am very proud [...] we did a very special movie; a very different movie. I think it is going to be very controversial because it is not a conventional movie [...] I think I've done something new for the industry.[6]

Despite such progressive claims, we find that the decision to hire Lynch was not based on the perceived idiosyncrasies of a director who worked against the restraints of genre ('The most original horror film ever made' to quote the promotional jargon for *Eraserhead*). It was Lynch's involvement with the classically structured *The Elephant Man* (and its recognition amongst the Academy no doubt) that drew De Laurentiis to Lynch. For *Dune*'s producers it was not so much the perception of Lynch as an artist that made him an appealing choice, it was the fact they saw him as a promising craftsman who might be prepared to 'join the team'. This line of argument is supported in declarations made in the same interview in which De Laurentiis remarked that she was 'very moved by *The Elephant Man*', and that with *The Elephant Man*, Lynch had 'proved that [he] could handle both character and special effects, and that was the kind of mixture I wanted to include in *Dune*'. And when asked by Auty if she'd seen *Eraserhead*, De Laurentiis insisted (laughing) that she only saw the film after she had begun working with Lynch; claiming, in fact, that she didn't 'know what [she] would have done if [she'd] seen it before'.[7] We are beginning to reveal then, a number of inconsistencies arising through the film's promotion, through which the identification of a creative source differed according to marketing and publicity contexts.

Generally speaking, the auteur picture has been perceived historically as one that rewrites, or works against, generic conventions and as such the reading of an auteur picture depends upon a shared understanding between producer and receiver of what those conventions are. Given these stipulations we can proceed by establishing how *Dune* had been promoted as an enclosed, or readerly, generic text. This will have wider importance too, since it will inform the reception of Lynch's *Dune* and how the author might function for pleasure against appreciations of generic elements.

Despite Lynch's limited control in this area, it was largely with respect to *Dune*'s mise en scène that the film was publicised and read as marking a departure for the science fiction blockbuster since, in many respects, it resists the polished technological look associated with the contemporaneous *Star Wars* cycle. In his essay 'Autoplastic and alloplastic adaptations in science fiction' (1983), Gary K. Wolfe showed that *Star Wars*, like *Dune* 'attempts to resolve the opposition of self and environment', by means of 'autoplastic and alloplastic fantasies'. In an autoplastic sense, the films share characteristics since the autoplastic dimensions of *Star Wars* are located in its desert, ice and jungle planets 'where the rebels live and are forced to adapt themselves to unpromising environments', and where the 'ancient Yoda survives by drawing on an inner power called "The Force"'. Against these thematic consistencies, *Dune* noticeably differs from *Star Wars* since 'the villainous Empire [in *Star Wars*] is consistently associated with alloplastic ('completely remaking environments to meet cultural needs') adaptations that include 'an entirely artificial planet called the "Death Star"' (Wolfe 1983: 67–69). There are clear contrasts to be found between the polished white interiors and high key lighting of the Death Star, the white plastic uniforms worn by the Stormtroopers and *Star Wars*' futuristic pageantry, and the expressionistic, medieval and industrial worlds of *Dune*.

The comparison between *Dune* and *Star Wars* is not an arbitrary one since it is clear that in a generic sense, *Dune* was a text that embodied many of the proven commercial formulas of the *Star Wars* cycle. Yet, like all genre films, event films (especially event films perhaps) have to be perceived as discernible in some way. In Ed Nana's tie-in book, *The Making of Dune* (1985), the film's difference (in respect of the technological excesses of *Star Wars*) is presented foremost in terms of its design and special effects, and in creative terms, through the exceptional endeavours of specialist individuals working in collaboration with Lynch.

This can be illustrated firstly with reference to Anthony Masters's production design. The interiors of the organic planet Caladan, incorporated rich decorative wood finishing while the regal planet Kaitain drew on palatial gold and jade, and the ornate and curving decoration associated with eighth–sixteenth-century Moorish architecture. The look of the planet Giedi Prime placed its emphasis on overcast Victorian black metal industrial design and green porcelain, and for the design of the hostile desert planet of Arrakis, Masters was influenced by Byzantine mosaics and ancient Egyptian architecture. The spacecraft and prop designs, meanwhile, were conceived of as organic (rather than technological) and took on what Masters described as 'insect-like appearance[s]' (Nana 1985: 47–64).

These infringements on generic rule may be pursued further through a consideration of *Dune*'s costume design, which is described by Bob Ringwood as 'a mixture of fantasy period costumes and fetish industrial costumes'. Ringwood had been hired (on the strength of his work on the 1981 medieval fantasy *Excalibur*) on the proviso that he must consider the costume for the four planets as industrial, dignified, military and earthy, and 'unlike anything [that] resembled a costume seen before in a science fiction movie'. The Emperor's Court costumes, for instance, were conceived of as a mixture of late-nineteenth-century and mid-seventeenth-century military costume. The Emperor's formal dress is described as 'exceedingly Victorian regal' while the Water Monks of Arrakis were dressed in religious hooded robes made from tied pipe and raw silk. The more industrial and organic costumes, such as those worn by fighting troops, were constructed of black rubber with the intent of appearing 'active yet sinister', while for the stillsuits (designed for the Fremen with the function of recycling body fluids into drinking water) Ringwood based his design on fetishist anatomical leather sculpture (Nana 1985: 65–78).

Nana's book also reported that *Dune* marked a departure from the science fiction event picture through an emphasis on characterisation rather than special effects. A number of *Dune*'s special optical effects, designed by 'visual wizard' Kit West, were relatively primitive since they relied not on such devices as stop-motion animation, blue-screen shots and rotoscoping (tracing live action with animation), but on the staging for the camera of 'physical effects'. Nana describes how it was West's job to 'create a host of eye-boggling stunts that can be carried out "live" while the cameras are running'. According to Nana, *Dune*'s physical effects were 'an almost mathematical endeavour, requiring technical savvy, imagination, ingenuity and an uncanny sense of timing'. The reader was told, in fact, that 'special effects are not constantly in the spotlight. Rather, they are subtly interwoven into the complex plotline to heighten its dramatic intensity. The characters and their adventures are the real focal points of the picture, while the special effects are used liberally to create a sense of realism' (Nana 1985: 139–40).

Marketing *Dune*

Dune's commercial properties were exploited, as they routinely are in science fiction event films, through various forms of tie-in merchandising. And while some of these pieces, including *Dune* action figures and models,[8] might appeal to *Dune* enthusiasts as collectables, it was the job of specialist publications aimed at *Dune* aficionados to reinforce Herbert's agency. Herbert's presence on the set, documented through publicity stills such as those featured in *The Making of Dune* book, and his general endorsement of the film, functioned to reassure *Dune* enthusiasts that the filmmakers had stayed true to Herbert's vision.

The sleeve for *The Making of Dune*, for instance, bannered it: 'The reality behind the fantasy! The story behind the spectacle! The filming of Frank Herbert's best-selling science fiction masterpiece!'. The sleeve also carried a photograph of Herbert and Lynch, the former in charge of a clapperboard featuring the film's title, accompanied by a quote attributed to Herbert: 'Tell the fans they're making the real *Dune*'. Herbert's endorsement is reiterated within the pages of the book with the book's author offering reassurances that 'the characters are exactly as [he had] envisioned them...sometimes even better' (Nana 1985: 35). Indeed, one suspects that it was because Lynch's status as auteur was not publicly established that his name was not emphasised (except in France where *Cahiers du Cinéma* had championed the Hollywood auteur some 30 years earlier and where the lobby poster bannered *Dune* 'un film de David Lynch')[9] in general promotions for the film.

In America, Britain and other European countries the film was sold in fact, as a 'Universal Pictures' event'. In the run up to *Dune*'s Christmas release, pre-publicity for the film, which appeared in British theatres in the form of lobby cards and fliers, promised a film 'beyond all experience, all imagination...the motion picture event of 1984' (see Dune Index at www. arrakis.co.uk). This emphasis was also utilised in the original promotional poster for the film that featured an illustration of Paul Atreides in a desert landscape, flanked by Chani, the female Fremen leader (and Paul's love interest) and an army of Fremen warriors. These figures were placed in a panoramic 'spacescape' featuring a distant planet and a flotilla of spaceships headed with text 'A world beyond your experience, beyond your imagination DUNE'. To emphasise *Dune*'s ambitions in scale and its novelty, the UK poster featured a quote from a review in *Newsweek* which referred to the film as a 'spellbinding saga of the future [that] towers over most futuristic epics. It is richer and stranger than just about anything the commercial cinema has to offer.'[10] The epic proportions of *Dune*, finally, were tagged in its theatrical trailer through which Herbert and De Laurentiis emerged as creative agents. Visually the trailer placed emphasis on the spectacular and

Dune promotional poster.

romantic elements of the film, while a ceremonious voice-over promised the following experience:

> You are about to enter a world where the unexpected and the unbelievable meet. Where kingdoms are built on earth that moves…and skies are filled with fire. Where a young warrior is called upon to free his people. A world that holds creation's greatest treasures and greatest terrors. A world where the mighty, the mad and the magical will have their final battle. Dune: a spectacular journey through the wonders of space from the boundaries of the incredible, to the borders of the impossible. Now, Frank Herbert's widely read, talked about and cherished masterpiece comes to the screen. Dino De Laurentiis presents *Dune*: a world beyond your experience and a world beyond your imagination.[11]

Writing Lynch's *Dune*

In spite of *Dune*'s creative team plan, it would be patently wrong to shelve *Dune* on the grounds that it is not an auteurist picture; that Lynch's signature did not come to bear on the reading of the film's style or its content. All the same, the general direction of our discussion so far has been to bring into dispute Lynch's status as the film's author on the documented evidence that:

1) he was part of a creative collaboration;
2) the producers wished to stay true to the essence of the source novel (in structural and thematic terms the filmed version of *Dune* would seem closer to Frank Herbert's *Dune* than 'David Lynch's Stunning Sci-Fi Spectacular');
3) despite pre-publicity that made claims for the film as a 'new departure', *Dune* was planned and articulated as a generic work; as a science fiction event picture rather than an auteur picture.

In dry empirical terms then, we might discard any Lynchian readings of *Dune* as little more than hermeneutic wish fulfilment and claim that any salient authorship is imagined rather than actual. But to retire on such a position does not help us account for the workings of the auteur as a preferred way of making sense of a text. Understood in these terms then, auteurism can be seen as an ideological (rather than scientific) operation through which the horizonal ontology of the text – be that formal, thematic and/or industrial – will trigger the search for an authorial voice from the predisposed reader.

Indeed, given that Lynch was yet to feature in promotion and publicity, critics tended to inscribe Lynch in *Dune* as a stylist (a *metteur-en-scène* rather than a true auteur under the terms of *la politique des auteurs*). *Films and Filming* carried a review that reported that 'Lynch has made of *Dune* an almost mythic, semi-religious fable, with a true sense of grandeur, the like of which the screen has not felt since the heady days of The Ten Commandments' (Sloman 1985). In conceding that 'the enormity of the production pretty well crushes his artistic distinctiveness', *Variety* still spoke of David Lynch's 'visually unique' film that 'holds the interest due to its abundant surface attractions' (Cart 1985). It is with these comments in mind that we turn our attention now towards the *personality of the text* that emerges in the retrospective readings of *Dune* that approached the film in the certain knowledge that Lynch was a true auteur.

It will come as little surprise to us that evidence of collaboration or concession making is seen as detrimental to an author's standing, since self-expression is an introverted business. We read that in accounts of *Dune* by Drazin, Le Blanc and Odell, and Woods, respectively: the 'producers' need for a marketable commodity' dictated that 'in being faithful to the Frank Herbert novel, Lynch accepted many of the absurdities that he might otherwise have questioned' (Drazin 1998: 36), that *Dune* is 'without doubt, Lynch's least satisfying film' and that Lynch was hampered by 'the preliminary problem of adapting someone else's story' (Le Blanc and Odell 2000: 34–35), and that *Dune* is 'only nominally "A David Lynch Film", in that touches of its director's obsessive imagination sporadically filter through before being neutralised by the dated, anonymous sweep of the traditional Hollywood epic' (Woods 2000: 65). But having reached agreement that *Dune* is the least Lynchian film in his oeuvre, biographical readings will still engage in the customary auteurist practice of seeking out intertextual associations with the director's other films.

It becomes apparent that *Dune* could not be discounted altogether since auteurist imprints of previous and future masterworks must be located in lesser, or supporting, texts. Nochimson (1997: 128), for instance, suggested that the planet Giedi Prime was 'in hindsight, the home of the mutilated masculinity as it is more powerfully defined in *Blue Velvet*', while for Drazin (1998: 37) 'the grotesque baron [Harkonnen] seems like a prototype for Frank [Booth] and the larger than life villains that would follow in Lynch's subsequent films'. Indeed, the reading of leading man, Kyle MacLachlan, as

Paul Atreides, vis-à-vis *Blue Velvet*'s Jeffrey Beaumont, illustrates very well how an author's personality must find its way into the text if that text is to rank as an authentic auteurist text.

As I have already mentioned, Lynch has suggested that he was drawn to *Dune* (in part) since the character of Paul is 'a typical Lynchian hero'; that is 'the sleeper who must awaken and become what he must become' (Rodley 1997: 116). But it was only following the release of *Blue Velvet* that MacLachlan (who also played a leading role as Special Agent Dale Cooper in the television series *Twin Peaks* and its cinematic prequel *Twin Peaks: Fire Walk with Me)* came to be viewed by the auteurist as Lynch's alter ego. This is not to say that the character of Jeffrey is not an archetypal Oedipal hero; rather, critics imbued Jeffrey with Lynchian mannerisms in a way that they did not with Paul. So while the writing of Lynch's legend accommodates inconsistent speculations upon the meanings in his films, we are able to see that certain horizonal principles must be agreed upon for a film to justly rank as the work of a true auteur.

It is important to know that *Dune* was MacLachlan's first screen performance and as such he constituted a blank page onto which a star persona could be written. MacLachlan could not be read into *Dune* on an intertextual level, in other words, since he had no screen history. Accidentally or not, such anonymity suited the wishes of the producers since the casting of MacLachlan removed the potential for hermeneutic interferences from previous films. Indeed, returning once more to the tie-in book, *The Making of Dune*, MacLachlan stresses his long kinship with the novel and particularly of course, the character of Paul: 'I don't know any character I feel closer to [...] When I was growing up I always thought of myself as Paul... "What would Paul do about this? What would Paul do about that"' (Nana 1985: 44). However, since Lynch only began to develop authorial status proper with the release of *Blue Velvet* (and as *Blue Velvet* is habitually read as an auteurist masterwork) it is at this point in time that MacLachlan begins to be read as the personification of the author himself rather than as a discrete character. The following passage, taken from Michael Atkinson's book *Blue Velvet* (1997: 22), underpins this tendency most visibly:

> Lynch found MacLachlan for *Dune*, and doubtlessly had hopes he could use
> him in *Blue Velvet*'s self-reflexive manner sometime after the lumbering,
> ill-planned sf fiasco had receded into the past. By using MacLachlan as his
> doppelganger, Lynch places himself and his pathologies in the centre of *Blue*

Velvet's mill wheel; although the film is easily recognizable as absolutely 'personal', MacLachlan's presence [...] tells us that Lynch knows it as well, and the film is some form of self-revelation, or self interrogation.

The provisional nature of the above statement is noticeable if measured against Lynch's indifferent take on the subject in which Lynch acknowledges certain exterior resemblances with MacLachlan, and the idea that MacLachlan 'took certain things' from his appearance (including the buttoned collar), but otherwise refutes the idea that Jeffrey/MacLachlan was ever intended as his ideological incarnation (Rodley 1997: 141). For the purposes of our argument, though, it is unimportant whether or not, or to what extent, Lynch intended MacLachlan to function as his alter ego. What I want to stress is the underlying rationale of Atkinson's judgement, which is based on the principle that evidence of agency must manifest itself in the auteurist text in a way that it does not in the genre picture.

Atkinson was not alone in this line of thinking. Chion, although his position on *Dune* is less hostile, also disapproved of the film since the viewer never comes to know what Paul represents because 'Lynch's own

Lynch and MacLachlan on the set of *Blue Velvet*.

view of his character is impossible to situate or determine […] he does not even have a viewpoint'. Chion (1996: 79–86) indeed, begins his analysis of *Blue Velvet* by stating that 'MacLachlan as Jeffrey makes us forget Paul Atreides'. Nochimson (1997: 102–30) alluded to this position too, when she proposed that 'dreams constitute the core of *Dune* and suggest what the film might have been had Lynch not been constrained to do a conventional treatment of Paul's destiny'. With Jeffrey, on the other hand, Nochimson followed Atkinson by suggesting that he be read as the 'Lynchian seeker […] whose discovery of the severed ear is significant in its revelation of cultural limits placed on the incipient seeker by both law enforcement and outlaws'. We have established then, that *Dune*'s meaning is dependent on corroborative sources and those who subscribe to the wisdom of authorial or auteurist essentialism will do so in defiance of logic. But we might want to ask now what a text like *Dune* shows us about the temperament of textual pleasure and the function of auteurism.

Authorship Pleasures

For Barthes, a text's meaning lay in its destination not its origin, and the manner in which we read determines how we will experience that text. In *The Pleasure of the Text*, Barthes speaks of 'tmesis', a rhythmic type of reading that an author cannot cater for. Tmesis is, in Barthes's description 'a seam or flaw resulting from a simple principle of functionality; it does not occur at the level of the structure of languages but only at the moment of their consumption' and 'it is the very rhythm of what is read and what is not read that creates the pleasure of the great narratives'. But for Barthes, there was the other system of reading (to which we might dispatch the above responses to *Dune*) that is the enemy to this preferred type of 'anecdotal' reading. Auteurism is in principle a deterministic criticism that *alludes* to the task of 'the winnowing out of truths'. But with the anecdotal reading method 'it is not (logical) extension that captivates' but rather 'the layering of significance' (Barthes 1975a: 11–12), that affords the higher state of blissful pleasure. For Barthes, then, the experience of bliss 'does not depend on a logic or understanding and on sensation', but should rather be understood as 'a drift, something both revolutionary and asocial [that] cannot be taken over by any collectivity, any mentality, any ideolect' (1975a: 23). In all cases though, the text of bliss must be understood by the reader to be disobedient in some way or other.

Barthes states that the text which offers this elevated state of drifting pleasure is one that will 'bring to crisis' the reader's 'relation with language' whereas the unexceptional, or static, text of pleasure 'comes from culture and does not break with it' (1975a: 14). But for a text to break with culture then there must exist a collective sense of what kinds of texts that culture routinely gives rise to. This collective sense is not obvious, but nor is it lacking (a situation that for Barthes, presumably, deserves commendation). Freud, in the preface to the Hebrew translation of *Totem and Taboo*, noted that he was 'completely estranged from the religion of his fathers' and that he could not 'take a share in nationalistic ideals'. Yet he still remarked that 'If the question were put to him: "Since you have abandoned all these common characteristics of your countrymen, what is left of you that is Jewish?" he would have to reply: "A very great deal, and probably its very essence"', even though he realised that he would be unable to 'express that essence clearly in words' (Freud 1950: ix). We might say, then, that the idea of culture – which a thesaurus search tells us might double for: civilisation, society, mores, background, traditions, ethnicity, customs, way of life, ethos, philosophy, nation and so on – can only exist in some notional state of equilibrium, even though that equilibrium is in reality contingent. In the context of this discussion, we can think of early auteurism this way, as a culture or ideology that exists within film criticism.

We are able though, to anchor early auteurism as a relatively fixed cultural paradigm; as a natural extension of our lifelong learning about authors who come into learned existence almost as soon as the child learns about stories. And, as Barthes had previously observed, the author is helpful (although not desirable) since, not unlike God, he is a means for making good the contradictions of existence that are made manifest in important texts. We can situate Barthes's ideas in line with the most logical development of French cultural criticism, which, in keeping with a modernistic commitment to progress, was attempting to move on from the totalising foibles of structuralism (and before that, authorial romanticism). Barthes was, in spite of everything, trying to take account of superior texts; texts that are 'greater than', or beyond readerly, but without succumbing to the pitfalls of determinism. A study such as ours might be inclined not to ponder the idea of ranking pleasure at all, since Barthes's model is such a shifting judgement that it appears to work against any kind of materialistic investigation (which would fit exactly with Barthes's hypothesis). We may have even sidestepped Barthes altogether, except that auteurism and writerly bliss do not deserve to be seen as wholly adversarial.

Auteurism foundered long ago on its narrow deterministic outlook. If we come to the text with an auteurist disposition, or even as a Lynch biographer with a horizon of expectation for a David Lynch film, then we will come in search of evidence of agency. If we proceed with Barthes, who said of criticism (1975a: 21) that it 'always deals with the text of pleasure, never the text of bliss', then we would appear to have little choice but to concur since the auteurist text will maintain a seemingly pre-determined threshold for meaning. But whether or not we bring an author with us to the text, we will anyway come with one set of cultural expectations or another and it is in how those horizons match up to the evidence of the text that pleasure or bliss (or pleasure and bliss) present themselves.

Hoberman, in his article entitled 'The end of science fiction' (1991: 206–10), first published in *The Village Voice* (1985) on *Dune*'s first cycle of release, was confronted, for instance, with a film that expanded his horizonal expectations for a science fiction event picture – a film 'steeped in an ancient, primordial nastiness that has nothing to do the sci-fi film as we currently know it'. In its narrative aspect, his assessment was fairly typical in that he viewed *Dune* as a film of 'frantic compression' and 'plagued with clumsy exposition'. And while he judged Lynch culpable by association, it was also Herbert and the film's novelistic elements that helped explain the film's 'morass of clichés', its 'laughable dialogue' and its 'pretentious terminology'. Hoberman, though, was much more stimulated in declaring that *Dune* didn't 'look like any science fiction film ever made' and that 'there are moments in this movie when you simply can't believe your eyes'. Indeed, it was Lynch – to the authorial disadvantage of Ringwood, Masters and ('special effects mechanical features modeler') Carlo Rambaldi (Nana 1985: 236–37) – who emerged; in the 'lysergic Jules Verne' style of 'dull [and] tarnished [...] weathered Deco patterns', the 'bosom suppressing gowns of 18th century Spanish infantas' and 'the film's most startling creature, a thing called the Spacing Guild Navigator [...] that talks through what can only be described as a withered vulva (typically shown in tight close-up) complete with clitoris' (Hoberman 1991: 206–10).

Hoberman's criticism does not read to me at all like mere pleasure so much as a manifest response to an experience that sits closer to the blissful reading processes Barthes described. It is in my view difficult to think of his commentary as 'contained' in any authorial sense; in this respect it comes across rather as anecdotal and even rhythmic. There might be disagreement on this point, but we can certainly see how the need to find a human repository for what are, after all, libidinal currents could be a means of taking control of such an experience. Barthes (1975a: 27), in fact, might well have agreed with our estimation since he acknowledged that 'in the text, in a way, *I desire* the author'.

It is clear to us that as public institution at least, the author has survived. Nowhere is this more patent than in the industrial context of post-classical cinema. And even if we do settle on Barthes's complaint that once an author has wooed us, and we subsequently come to the text with that 'biographical person' in hand, then the rhythmic frisson cannot be recaptured, we overlook the crucial point made by Freud in 'Beyond the pleasure principle' (1995: 611) that while 'novelty is always the condition of enjoyment' the 'compulsion to repeat' is always a condition of pleasure. We will further this discussion now in turning our attention to the reception of an auteurist work proper, Lynch's contested masterpiece, *Blue Velvet*.

CHAPTER 4

Critical Theory and 'Cruel Jokes': Principles of Ethics and Pleasure, and the Reception of *Blue Velvet*

In the previous chapter, and throughout the course of this volume, we come across examples that show us that the auteurist generally prefers to be self-ruling and free from the constraints of factual accounts of authorial activity. Paul de Man, in fact, pointed towards the potential for the kind of writerly author function we have identified, when he spoke of the seductive spell of the aesthetic text, that knows how to hasten in the reader 'a eudemonic judgment that can displace and conceal values of truth and falsehood' (Jauss 1982: vii–xxv). In his account of Ozu, on the other hand, Bordwell (1988: 163) identified a more austere approach to the aesthetic text when he called upon Wimsatt and Beardsley's 'notorious' concept of 'intentional fallacy', which, pre-empting Barthes to some degree, recommended that while an author's intentions might help in 'explaining the historical constitution of the art work', that intention was in fact 'irrelevant to judging or interpreting the work's aesthetic effects'. Given these two positions, the author then becomes effectively a choice; someone to be picked up or discarded according to the motivations of the writer. It is with regard to the latter, and the *alleged rebuttal* of authorship, that this chapter takes forward our discussion of Lynch.

We must, in a reception study of Lynch, be prepared to recognise (as we might with other auteurs) that his films can have extended effect outside an undeveloped, or 'early', auteurist paradigm. In this regard we may turn our attention to receptions of *Blue Velvet* as grouped under the heading

'Critical Theory'. Critical theory seemed to offer a route away from the humanist drawbacks of early auteurism since it was, or is, steered by the dogmas of structuralism and post-structuralism that propose, respectively, that the author be seen as an agent composed through language (rather than the celestial 'author god' that Barthes (1977: 147) described), or that he or she be overlooked in the reading act altogether. *Blue Velvet* proved a difficult film to come to grips with for those engaged in the struggle for sex and class equities. While some scholars applauded *Blue Velvet*'s formal and thematic bravura, others viewed the film as a textual snare designed to trap the theoretician and to entice a state of moral uncertainty. Indeed, Lynch, had his testimony been allowed, would have only confused matters more, since he claimed that *Blue Velvet* was not intended as a critique (as feminist scholars such as Cynthia Fuchs had read it), but was instead 'a subconscious thing' where 'words [and] rational thinking [would have got] in the way' (Rodley 1997: 140).

Lynch's position in these accounts offered a substantial theoretical challenge, not least since the foundations of such arguments have tended to rely on the belief that Hollywood films function as part of an insidious propagandist mechanism. It was enough, therefore, for Marxist Fredric Jameson (1989) to decide that *Blue Velvet* was a seemingly authorless, generic piece of popular culture showing a postmodern characteristic that trivialised deviant social activities such as sadomasochism, drug abuse, murder and organised crime. On the other hand, feminist critiques – which at that time were founded on psychoanalytical perceptions of the workings of the cinematic apparatus and, especially, Laura Mulvey's (1999: 841) evocative observations on the male's 'voyeur[istic] and fetishistic fascination' with Hollywood films – were more attuned to *Blue Velvet*'s formal and structural methods. In these accounts *Blue Velvet* was held up less as a generic work and much more as a text of aesthetic character.

The feminist reception of *Blue Velvet* in particular shows us that the film was a highly ambiguous proposition; an art film crowded with formal and thematic contradictions that seemed to address questions about the nature of cinematic truth and how the cinematic apparatus positions us as gendered spectators. Indeed, although feminist scholars were not, by-and-large, in the business of establishing intertextual author citations, *Blue Velvet* was still approached as an expression of a male ego that appeared to reveal an insider's knowledge of many of feminism's theoretical concerns.

Our analysis of *Blue Velvet* raises important questions pertaining to conflicts between the pursuit of pleasure and attitudes towards ethical responsibility. It is to Freud that we will turn in taking account of how Lynch 'the artist' operated in this taxing postmodern relationship.

We have established that on its release in 1986, *Blue Velvet* emerged as a cultural event; 'a must for buffs and seekers of the latest hot thing' as *Variety* billed it (Cart 1986). And we have established that it was *Blue Velvet*, Lynch's fourth feature, which secured him a position within the pantheon of new Hollywood auteurs (Pauline Kael famously declaring (1986) that Lynch could be the 'first popular surrealist – a Frank Capra of dream logic'). But *Blue Velvet* was also a divisive film. The *National Review*, for instance, carried a review by John Simon in which he argued that the 'harvest of laurels' garnered by *Blue Velvet* was wholly unmerited. Simon (1986) described the film as 'a piece of mindless junk'; a film that did no more than strive for 'sexual arousal'. And further that whereas 'true pornography, which does not pretend to be anything else, has at least a shred of honesty to recommend it', *Blue Velvet* was a 'dishonest' film that only 'pretend[ed] to be art'. Simon concluded with the view that 'sadomasochism, voyeurism, latent homosexuality, fetishism and whatnot would be fine if the goal were insight rather than titillation and shock'.

The themes of artistic glorification, textual pleasure and ethical dispute are the focal points for this chapter. Indeed, by extending our study to encompass the film's scholarly reception (although not to the neglect of its public standing), we are able to attempt a textual historicity that tenders observed outcomes on the social role of the artist and on the relationship between ethics and pleasure. For the most part, we will be looking at receptions of the film that come out of the field of critical theory and, except for the inclusion of one example for reasons that will become clear, feminist/psychoanalytical discourse, since it is in these receptions that 'the *Blue Velvet* problem' was most sharply brought into focus.

We have already seen that artistic and ethical concerns also dominated public discussions of the film. But in the public domain, the issue of authorship was never at stake. As we will recall from our earlier discussion, we took up Staiger's 'authorship as origin approach' (the approach whereby 'the author is conceptualized as a free agent, untroubled philosophically or linguistically – although rational individuals might debate interpretation' (Staiger 2003: 30)) to account for the auteurism that dictates in the public sphere. Critical theory, on the other hand, comes out of a context of late 1960s Paris, where radical reforms within French intellectual life, such as those we have just encountered through Barthes, challenged the accepted wisdom of authorship studies and that of the creator as governor of meanings. Critical theory, therefore, might incline to view an author like Lynch either as myth, and/or his death as given. In practice, though, this is no more than a rule of thumb, while in some special instances exceptions have even been made for authorial determinism in readings whereby the lived experience of marginalised groups is understood in a shared history between audience and author (e.g. Medhurst 1991; Mercer 1991). Agency, however, becomes all the more problematic when author and recipient do not share in those lived struggles and when the author and theorist appear to meddle in one another's affairs.

With *Blue Velvet*, indeed, there was a strong suspicion in some quarters that Lynch, the newest darling of the cineliterate community, had set out deliberately to undermine feminist film theory. Lesley Stern (1993), for instance, described a film that was 'littered with "psychoanalytical tropes," [with] scenarios almost encased in quotation marks', and even went so far as to introduce an author/patient; theorist/analyst analogy through which she warned 'the patient might desire the analyst's ear but the analyst might be seduced by the tales that the patient tells, tales that might be cruel jokes'.

Just as the term 'auteurism', or to be branded an 'auteurist', tells us nothing of the subtleties of approaches to film and authorship, the intellectual allegiances and intricacies of 'critical theory' are undoubtedly such, that it is quite possible that the theorists to whom I refer below might, for reasons unbeknownst to me, harbour justified grievances at being grouped under this kind of banner heading. In pre-empting any censure, I will qualify my use of the term here as a means only of accounting for a collection of academic papers and essays that are associated in their critique of societal inequities (either upheld or challenged through cinema), and for whom 'David Lynch's *Blue Velvet*' presented a cultural and authorial predicament. I will in fact be referring to a total of eight papers published in the decade between 1988 and 1998. Seven of these, authored by feminist scholars, are connected principally through the themes of gender relations and Freudian psychoanalysis. The other, written by Jameson, takes a critical approach that is informed by the dialectics of class struggles within capitalism. We will begin with Jameson, since his essay sets up the overarching themes for this chapter.

Blue Velvet and Cinematic Realism

There was agreement amongst the scholarly community that *Blue Velvet* was a film that encapsulated the mood of a 1980s postmodern art cinema. As such, and while still maintaining firm ties to narrative, *Blue Velvet* offered no proverbial or symbolic exit points and thus failed to present any apparent logic or insight. In the film, our adolescent hero Jeffrey Beaumont and his virginal sweetheart Sandy Williams are diametrically cast against the demonic villain Frank Booth and his victim, the sexually abused torch singer Dorothy Vallens. The teenage sweethearts muse over the mysteries of life and love with an incorruptible naiveté. Jeffrey asks, 'Why are there people like Frank? Why is there so much trouble in this world?' Sandy tells Jeffrey of her dream in which, 'the world was dark because there wasn't any robins', but then, 'all of a sudden thousands of robins were set free and they flew down and brought this blinding light of love'. Frank's invective, meanwhile, is relentless: 'Let's fuck. I'll fuck anything that moves', 'Don't say *please*, fuck head', and so on.

If these character binaries lacked plausibility, then *Blue Velvet*'s composition confronted expectations for temporal realism too. If we pick out certain details in *Blue Velvet*'s mise en scène we can tell that the film is clearly not a period drama even if the prevailing mood is one of the 1950s American small town. Our sense of historical specificity is confused through the coexistence of 1950s American small-town iconography (white picket fences, skies of brilliant blue, neatly manicured lawns and hedges, street-corner diners and hardware stores and comely public servants) and the 1980s setting (the technology, vehicles, telephones, guns and cameras are modern day).

If the spectator's historical point of reference is upset through such anomalies, structurally, too, causal relations are only ostensibly logical. This is because *Blue Velvet*'s causal chains are destabilised through the introduction of strategies that can make us question the truth of what we witness. In one clear example, Jeffrey awakens in abrupt distress on his bed following Dorothy's rape ordeal (which I will come to in good time) perhaps encouraging the idea of dreams, or, for that matter, dreams within dreams, since it is able to imply that our hero might have dreamed the horrendous events in which he has just been involved. This proposition, though, is confused; firstly because the narrative develops according to normal causal relations that confirm that the rape ordeal did occur, and secondly, because

CRITICAL THEORY AND 'CRUEL JOKES' 69

in his encounter with Dorothy, Jeffrey is cut on his left cheek with a large kitchen knife. When Jeffrey wakes however, the attentive spectator will have noticed that his cheek is unscarred (thus implying that these events have indeed been dreamed). Yet in a later scene, where Jeffrey is watching Dorothy's performance in the *Slow Club*, a scar is visible (while it is again absent in other scenes).

There is a case to be made here, then, for a structural organisation based on dream logic rather than on the principles of realist storytelling. So unless one sees these and other peculiarities (such as the often commented upon mechanical robin featured in the closing scene) as shoddy craftsmanship, it logically follows that there must be a degree of eloquence at play. And faced with a text which has such premeditated characteristics on show, it is normal for the inclined spectator to seek textual mastery through authorial qualification.

Arising from the contexts of structuralism and post-structuralism, critical theory is apt to sidestep authorial romanticism; to view authors (if at all) as constituted by language rather than beneficiaries of godly inspiration. Even so, in Lynch's case, we find an author who is strongly disinclined to discuss causality in his films, preferring to speak of his work in terms of 'moods', 'abstractions' and 'feelings'. For Lynch 'a film is its own thing and in an ideal world [...] film should be discovered knowing nothing – nothing added to it and nothing subtracted from it' (Cousins 1999). This worldview was fleshed out in his discussion on *Blue Velvet* with Rodley (1997: 140):

> *Rodley*: The movie does seem to display or illustrate, almost perfectly, certain Freudian concepts and theories – and in an extreme undiluted way. Was that intentional?
> *Lynch*: My reasoning mind didn't ever stop and say 'What the hell am I doing?' That's why I keep saying that making films is a subconscious thing. Words get in the way. Rational thinking gets in the way. It can really stop you cold. But when it comes out in a pure sort of stream, from some other place, film has a great way of giving shape to the subconscious. It's just a great language for that.

If an artist is to justify their standing in the traditional modernist understanding of the term, then they should offer a potential route to social and self-enlightenment through their creative labours. And, accordingly, it is the search for evidence of dialogic properties that governs judgements in Marxist interpretations. Marxist critiques of postmodernism were buoyed to a marked extent by the writings of Jameson, whose structural analysis of *Blue Velvet* is governed by generic factors. Firstly, the raw issue for Jameson (as it is, indeed, with feminist readings) is one of truth(s): how does *Blue Velvet*, as a cinematic representative of postmodern culture, confuse literal or symbolic routes to social self-awareness and why might Lynch's agency be passed over in Jameson's pejorative account of the film?

Given modernism's historical association with the avant-garde, Jameson's basic objection to postmodern culture is located in its appetite for nostalgia and pastiche. He signalled his critical stance in his landmark essay 'The deconstruction of expression', later extended in 'Post-modernism: or the cultural logic of late capitalism', first published in *New Left Review* in 1984. The bottom line for Jameson was the idea that artistic self-expression should be offset by a wider sense of the travails of the oppressed social subject. As he wrote, 'the very concept of expression presupposes...some separation within the subject, [and] often cathartically, that "emotion" is then projected out and externalized, as gesture or cry' (1994: 1078). Since there can be no artwork without an artist, it follows that under Jameson's system of rules a perception (be that studied or imagined) of an author's life, however equivocal, is impossible to detach from the classification and judgement of the author's artworks.

This point is an important one since in political critiques the author, or the absence of an author, serves utilitarian (as well as hermeneutic) functions. This being so, authorship is contingent rather than manifest in the sense that any calling on authorial say-so rests upon the ethical outlook of the theorist and whether the artist in question is perceived as an ally or antagonist. In Jameson's assessment of *Blue Velvet*, Lynch's agency is overlooked, which supports the point I am making that a generic postmodern culture is socially more insidious than poetic high culture.

We will see shortly that there were different, if overlapping, priorities for feminist criticisms, and Lynch could not be so easily brushed aside. But through his generic reading, Jameson argued that *Blue Velvet*'s lack of inner truth revealed itself only as pastiche (of 1950s popular American culture). Additionally, Jameson (1989: 529) felt that the film's unrealistic representations of good and evil amounted to no more than a 'tired and antiquated binary opposition between virtue and vice' that was of itself a representative of a 1980s postmodern film style that married the 'high elegance of nostalgia films' with 'grade-B simulations of iconoclastic punk films'. Jameson's pessimistic assessment of *Blue Velvet* required, then, that the film's hyperrealism be understood as somehow unfelt and calculated, and *Blue Velvet* was positioned as a companion of other generic films – *Something Wild* (1986) in Jameson's example.

Jameson did, though, acknowledge that in an 'orthodox textbook way' *Blue Velvet* could be (mis)read as 'very "dialectical" indeed' since the film might 'mobilise anxieties about rape'. However, he believed that it would be 'a great mistake' to read the film 'as a kind of protofeminist denunciation of patriarchy' or a 'protopolitical protest'. This was because the potentially antithetical mixing of high elegance nostalgia with punk does not result in synthesis but, rather, the film's 'aesthetic contradiction becomes the thing in itself' (Jameson 1989: 527). Jameson's complaint, then, is that the film's style, and any pleasure we might derive from that, trivialises its content; the subject matter, in other words, is not treated with the appropriate formal asceticism.

The events that Jameson describes above occur in the scene in which Jeffrey semi-secretly witnesses (Dorothy is aware of Jeffrey's presence while Frank is not) the sadomasochistic assault/rape on/of Dorothy by Frank. We will come back to Jameson one more time a little later on, but it is the depiction of these events that, with very good reason, proved most challenging for feminist critiques of the film. And it is a consideration of the critical reception of this scene in particular (although not exclusively) that brings Lynch into our discussion.

But before we proceed, let us come back to the discussion from the previous chapter relating to Barthes's ideas on textual bliss and the practice of 'tmesis'. Barthes, we will recall, located the blissful pleasures of tmesis in the rhythm of reading and it was, for him, what is skipped; 'what is read and what is not read that creates the pleasure of the great narratives' (1975a: 23). Yet, without exception, readings of *Blue Velvet* paused, at length more often than not, to consider the ethical implications of the primal scene. I have yet to read an account of the film that does not do this. But what should we make of this fact? We could assign it the lowly status of pleasure (if our ego will permit the thought of pleasure at all) since according to Barthes this is all that is on offer through criticism. But the meaning of these events is so ambiguous and so contested – so writerly, in fact – that the primal scene I think must hint at something more about the nature of textual pleasure.

As we have just seen, for Jameson the act of comprehension in *Blue Velvet* is understood as given, but for feminist film scholars *Blue Velvet* was a more problematical text that under closer formal scrutiny was not so readily intelligible. As Cynthia Fuchs (1989) pointed out, with *Blue Velvet* 'normal structures of signification seem[ed] untrustworthy'. So, different but connected conflicts of interest arise if the theorist is concerned primarily with gender conflicts. This ambivalence arises chiefly out of the critical legacy of Laura Mulvey's illustrious polemic 'Visual pleasure and narrative cinema' (1999; first published 1975) that by the mid-1980s came to dominate discussions on gendered spectatorship and the workings of 'cinema as apparatus'. As such, feminist writings were much more tuned in to *Blue Velvet*'s formal and structural patterns than Jameson was.

As we have already established, within critical theory authorial intentionality, where it does not involve a sense of shared history, would be deemed naïve and outdated; a romantic analysis that has no merit in a progressive, post-structural interpretive act. But, following in the vein of Stern, Jane M. Shattuc (1992) suggested that *Blue Velvet* seemed to set out to bait 'the moral logic of feminism'. There was, then, a perception of dialogue between author and theorist. Although not everyone bought into this view of causality, and while Lynch's worldview and intertextual associations with his other works were of little significant consequence in feminist receptions, his presence/absence as author still gave noticeable shape to these critiques. Put more plainly, *Blue Velvet* was essentially understood as an artwork produced by a male artist, and as a premeditated (rather than expressionistic) artwork at that.

In respect of Lynch's position in these discussions, we can begin to separate our groups. Stern, like Jameson, ostensibly treats *Blue Velvet* as a generic work, and since artwork and artist go hand-in-hand, like Jameson, she would seem to have no practical need to cite Lynch's name. So although Stern does not cite Lynch by name (in the vein of Jameson, she addressed the film as one of 'these kind of films [that] operate on an economy of detachment') she still approached the film as a 'snare' that entailed 'a conception of the analyst, who is here invoked as a textual presence, as the mother "presumed to know"'. In the scene in which Dorothy is shown naked and beaten wandering the neighbourhood, and crying '*He* put his disease in me' (my emphasis), Stern was alerted 'not simply to a dynamic being played out between the dramatis personae of the film but to a dynamic involving the analyst'. 'What is being manifested here', she argued 'is an infantile sadistic desire to contaminate the analyst/mother by implanting foreign bodies, or transferring symptoms (poison)' (Stern 1993). Stern's understanding is, then, that *Blue Velvet* was the 'diseased' product of a man ('*He*') and the production of the film itself an act of malicious transference from man to woman.

This position shares in the conviction that *Blue Velvet* be viewed as a pernicious, generic film that is representative of a wider tendency in postmodern culture. Shattuc also fell into line with this estimation but, like the other feminist receptions of the film I discuss below, she acknowledged Lynch as creator of *Blue Velvet* (and even established loose intertextual associations with *Twin Peaks*, the 1990s postmodern television event that established Lynch as a high-profile public figure). With the exception of Lynne Layton (1994), whose essay marks the point of divergence in our analysis, we might, though, think of these acknowledgements of causality as only that; as acknowledgements and annotations rather than meaningful auteurist undertakings. Not that this fact is any less significant for the development of our own discussion.

Like all commentators, Shattuc had picked up on the film's shocking restaging of the 'primal scene', so called since it seemed to re-enact the moment in Freud's Oedipal trajectory when the child spies upon his copulating parents. As Mulvey noted (1996: 142) in her reading of the film 'the child interprets the scene as one of violence, even sadism, in which the father, the stronger partner, carries out a brutal attack on the mother, the weaker'. Read in symbolic terms, and through the cipher lens of psychoanalytic discourse, Frank, who carries out the sadomasochistic assault on Dorothy in front of the spying Jeffrey (who is hiding in the closet), stands in as the child's father surrogate (since his biological and mute father has been hospitalised). And by association, Dorothy features as the mother figure he so desires all for himself. The scene is also organised around a series of shifting cinematic looks and sexual power plays: firstly Dorothy over Jeffrey (who she holds at knifepoint) – 'Get undressed, I want to see you', 'Don't move ... don't look at me', 'Don't touch me or I'll kill you' – and then Frank over Dorothy – 'Don't you fuckin' look at me', 'spread your legs ... wider ... now show it to me', 'Baby wants to fuck'.

But even if a different, potentially multiple cinematic gaze was to emerge (in the first part of this scenario at least) – and while Shattuc echoed the general view that 'Dorothy's use of the knife does empower her' – she took issue with those critics who 'overwhelmingly legitimised the film's use of sexual violence as indicative of a new filmic form', and wherein 'aesthetic pleasure reigns over social consequence'. Her criticism, indeed, echoed many of the ethical warnings Jameson had voiced when she wrote:

> *Blue Velvet*'s violence emanates from two central opposing traditions in postmodernism: the Oedipal structure of the classical realist narrative and the iconoclastic play on forms of modernism. These two traditionally oppositional forms – mass culture and modernism – when combined may engender a disorienting sexual confusion on the part of the spectator, but they also break down moral boundaries and celebrate the perversity of the unprecedented sexual violence against women. (Shattuc 1992)

It was Frank's assault on Dorothy that introduced the theme of the primal fantasy (or pre-Oedipal fantasy depending on one's point of view). Frank, who is shown inhaling a substance through an on oxygen mask, is placed on his knees, between a seated Dorothy's parted legs, as he moans, 'Mummy' repeatedly. Dorothy reassures Frank, 'Mummy loves you', as he pleads 'Baby wants to fuck'. Then (in what appears to be drug induced thraldom), Frank rages 'Get ready to fuck', warns Dorothy once more 'Don't you fuckin' look at me' (he issues this threat on no less than three occasions) before punching her full in the face. Rather than recoil in pain, however, Dorothy is shown through a close shot in a state of sexual rapture. In this scene we also witness Frank violently force some of the lining from Dorothy's torn velvet gown into her vagina as she writhes in pain before he performs a violent simulation of intercourse. Having seemingly, and hurriedly, reached orgasm, Frank climbs off Dorothy, flexes his hand/fist and warns one last time 'Don't you fuckin' look at me' before again punching her in the face (Dorothy is once more framed in her state of rapture).

Fuchs was one of the theorists who found progressive qualities in the scene's apparent lack of pellucidity. She described, 'David Lynch's *Blue Velvet*' as, 'a movie of our time'; a film in which, 'moral boundaries and power relations have become multiple, fluid, disturbingly indistinct'. 'Linking perception with perversion', she continued, 'viewers are held responsible for their visions' and, 'included in this category "viewers" are the theorists and critics who determine a closed system of reading in which the reader/viewer maintains anonymity inculpability' (Fuchs 1989). Lynda K. Bundtzen (1998), meanwhile, saw Frank's actions as 'the persistent frustration of the infant who can never re-enter the mother's body'. Dorothy's 'wounded maternal body' was read as 'the site and sight of [Frank's] impotence, castration, a body that might deprive him of autonomy and manhood if left unmastered by aggression'. Mulvey (1996: 44–45), too, thought that Frank's assault on Dorothy was 'closer to Freud's vision of infantile sexuality as polymorphously perverse, than to adult genital sexuality'. His 'orality, voyeurism, sadism, [his] acting out of the child's understanding of the female body as castrated, and finally, and most significantly, his fetishistic fixation on the blue velvet' represented Frank's '"regression" to babyhood (his desire to "go back home")'. And although rather more ambivalent towards the film's potential for dialectic plaudits, Barbara Creed (1988) suggested that the voyeuristic element of the 'primal fantasy is aligned to masochism' (over eroticism) 'not only is the scene difficult to watch [...] but the spectator is also punished for watching in that events which unfold before the eyes of the "innocent" viewer/child are both shocking and violent'.

What we can see in the above examples is that despite a critical approach that springs from philosophical contexts that are sceptical of authorial readings, an author will be an accepted presence in texts that are aesthetic in character, even if this is only an ethereal presence. We might even say that the tendency to only annotate Lynch's name is merely a process of default for the theorist and in pursuing my own line of argument I am clutching at straws. But this is not so.

Staiger (2003: 29) has argued that 'taking studies of the author off the table can eliminate the politically crucial question of causality for texts', which, she continued, is 'highly undesirable from the point of view of critical theory'. It would be thwarting my own aims to speculate on how Stern's reading of Blue Velvet, for instance, would differ if she had perceived the author as a woman. Her reading is gender specific and, in any case, this would be a rather fractious proposition since Blue Velvet was not, after all, written and directed by a woman. But, to return to the point I made earlier, the problem remains that critical readings of the film will invoke certain judgements through even the most rudimentary author imaginings. If we come to the film in the knowledge that it was directed (and written) by Lynch (a man), or if we even seek out this knowledge subsequently, then this closes off feminist readings pertaining to notions of 'Us'. We are beginning to see, then, that there are obstructions in the way of a direct drive for change through theoretical and critical developments that seek, or have sought, to leave the author to the past.

If we come back to Jameson's essay one last time we can find an interesting detail. I have established that Jameson read *Blue Velvet* as a generic work. But in the midst of his discussion he described Jeffrey's father's seizure as 'an act of God which is peculiarly an act of scandalous violence within the peaceful American small town [and] is positioned by David Lynch (also director of *Eraserhead*) within the more science fiction horizon of the Darwinian violence of all nature'. We could represent this sentence, indeed, without altering its meaning at all within the context of Jameson's wider discussion: 'an act of God which is peculiarly an act of scandalous violence within the peaceful American small town [and] is positioned [...] within the more science fiction horizon of the Darwinian violence of all nature' (Jameson 1989: 534). Since this reference to Lynch serves no wider function in respect of Jameson's contentions, and since there are no other references to Lynch or his other films, the utterance of his name must be thought of as a case of parapraxes, a 'Freudian slip' of the tongue or the pen. As Freud described it (1991: 70), parapraxes are 'not chance events but serious mental acts; they have a sense; they arise from concurrent action – or perhaps rather, the mutually opposing action – of two different intentions'. Based on Freud's evidence, we may reasonably introduce the idea that the need for an author might represent an instinctual manifestation that might be suppressed, but cannot be expunged.

The Artist as Creator

One feminist writer to meet Lynch head on in her reading of *Blue Velvet* is Layton, who proposed that (1994) 'a possible political interpretation arises from the fact that the 1950s and 1980s mark a period of development of our real hero, David Lynch' and the film, thus, offers 'a historicized parable of male development'. Recognising that *Blue Velvet* had 'stirred up a number of critical controversies relevant to feminist film criticism', Layton was interested in the idea of 'male trouble' which, she argued, involved a focus shift that was 'in part a move from Oedipal to pre-Oedipal dynamics' (1994: 375) and the male child's dependence on the mother. Her proposition stems from 'the fact that Frank's narcissistic rage has become a staple of contemporary mainstream and avant-garde filmmaking [which] suggests that these dynamics operate on the cultural as well as on the individual level'. Layton identified a total of four fields of potential 'crises in dominant male development'. The second, third and fourth of these arrive in the shape of: 1) 'the challenge to the dominance of heterosexuality' through the rise of the gay and lesbian movements; 2) the challenge 'to the dominance of whiteness' that is brought about by 'the civil rights movements, then by Vietnam and other Third World liberation struggles and now by the demand of multiculturalism'; and 3) the decline of 'the USA as an economic power and [...] the threat of a unified Europe' (Layton 1994: 388–90). But it is a perceived anxiety in gender roles that is at the root of her investigation.

Layton argued, in fact, that 'the anxiety that Lynch is such a master of generating with images and sounds', was a reflection of 'the heightened anxieties experienced by many men at this historical moment'. She attributed this anxiety in part to 'gender identity and gender roles' and to 'threats to the traditional ways' in which 'dependency and autonomy have been split between the genders' (1994: 392). In respect of the assaults on Dorothy, meanwhile, Layton drew on the work of Nancy Chodorow, whose book *The Reproduction of Mothering* (1978) represented 'an attempt to understand how the patterns of childrearing in the 1950s led to a situation in which heterosexual men and women, by virtue of their self structure, could not fulfill each others needs'. Layton proceeded thus (1994: 389):

> Her story, located in suburban USA, where Jeffrey Beaumont's story also takes place, features overinvolved mothers deprived of outlets for their desire other than their children, and largely absent fathers [...] Nurture, caretaking, emotion, dependence all becomes associated with females. Father absence prevents the boy from identifying with these attributes in a like other, which [...] leads to an Oedipal theory and reality that centres on competition and hostility rather than connection and care. The road to male gender identification involves disidentifying not only with the mother but everything that has been associated with her. This, Chodorow argues, is the characteristic psychic constellation of the heterosexual middle-class white male who came of age in the 1960s and 1970s [...] thus, the psychic constellation involves a lack of fathering and the eroticisation of dependency needs, as well as the expectation that mother has no other interest but her children. The pain caused by the absence of a nurturant father (The Sandman) is disavowed, and mother is blamed for all wounds.

If we take a closer look at Lynch's biography we can see that the above profile situates Lynch historically and geographically but otherwise we are presented with some less secure outcomes. Lynch was born in Missoula, Montana in 1946. His father worked as a Research Scientist for the Government's Department of Agriculture. His mother was indeed a housewife although she had gained a degree (Lynch's parents met at Duke University) and worked in some capacity as a language tutor (which suggests that she might have had interests other than her children). Because of his father's work, the Lynch family had moved five times (Sandpoint, Idaho, Spokane, Washington, Durham, North Carolina, Boise, Idaho and Alexandria, Virginia) by the time David was 14. There is nothing in Lynch's biographies, meanwhile, to suggest one way or another that his father was a physical or emotional absentee, although Lynch has referred to his father as an 'innocent' (Cousins 1999), which may invite connotations of a repressed, fatalistic character. He speaks fondly and respectfully of both parents and describes his childhood generally as troubled but not unhappy: 'I think every child has things they see, that affect them, and it's nobody's fault. It's just the way it is. It's just the way kids' minds work. It's maybe 75 per cent dream, 25 per cent reality' (Rodley 1997: 1–30).

If we are persuaded by the argument that *Blue Velvet* represents a reproach of his mother, this is not to say necessarily (or, perhaps, solely) that it is under the circumstances Layton/Chodorow describe. Freud remarked, for instance (1991: 337–38), that 'the position of a child in the family order is a factor of extreme importance in determining the shape of his later life and should deserve consideration in every life-history'. We learn from his biography, in fact, that Lynch is the eldest of three children (a brother and a sister) and as Freud also noted 'a child who has been put into second place by the birth of a brother or sister, and who is now for the first time almost isolated from his mother, does not easily forgive her this loss of place; feelings which in an adult would be described as greatly embittered arise in him and are often the basis of permanent estrangement' (1991: 337–38). There are other details in Lynch's biography, meanwhile, that suggest that he successfully, if not conventionally, dealt with the libidinal detachment from his mother and the authoritarian separation from his father (assuming he had been subservient to him). Under a post-structural reading paradigm, these details may be dismissed as mere speculation, but we can still use psychoanalysis and the author biography, to gain a more empirical understanding of what a film like *Blue Velvet* might mean on an individual and societal level.

We saw in Chapter 2 that although Lynch is famed as a filmmaker he was first and foremost an artist who arrived at filmmaking through a formal education in fine art. If we stay with Freud, this creates certain nuances once we appreciate the *text as being destined for an audience* – as, of course, a commercial film is. We would be wrong to assume, in other words, that the text offers a transparent topography of its creator's unconscious mind. For our purposes, the key point in Lynch's biography comes when he describes the realisation that he wanted to become a painter:

> We'd moved to Virginia [which ages him at around 15 or 16 years old] and I didn't know what I was going to do [as a career]. I didn't have a clue except I just liked painting. My father was a scientist so I thought I was going to be a scientist. […] I met my friend Toby Keeler in the front yard of my girlfriend's house – Linda Styles. And Toby did two things: he told me that his father was a painter, which completely changed my life, and he also stole my girlfriend! So I went to visit [Toby's] father's studio in Georgetown, and his father was a really cool guy [and that he had devoted his life to painting] thrilled my soul. And so I became friends with his father Bushnell Keeler – and that decided this course for painting, 100 per cent right there. (Rodley 1997: 9)

If we follow Freud's observations on artists in his account 'Symptom formations of neurosis', it seems likely that these two events (the stealing away of his girlfriend and becoming an artist) were pivotal moments in his development. According to Freud, the artist – 'in rudiment an introvert' and 'not far removed from neurosis'[1] – 'desires to win honour, power, wealth, fame and the love of women; but he lacks the means for achieving these satisfactions'. Like any such 'unsatisfied man' the artist then 'turns away from reality and transfers all his interest and his libido too, to the wishful construction of his life as phantasy whence the path might lead to neurosis'. But the true artist, one who is able to find 'a path back to reality' (Freud 1991: 423) through artistic endeavours, is able to avoid neurosis via these means.

Artists, Audiences and Pleasure

I will come back to the above point but, to recap, we have established four general attitudes towards *Blue Velvet*, some of which overlap but all of which are confronting ethical uncertainties. Firstly, Lynch's sadistic fantasy involves a punishment of the maternal figure and the root of this neurosis is located in childhood experience. Secondly, and this one succumbs to sadistic connotations too, *Blue Velvet* carries a calculated prank: an attempt to goad the film theorist and to entice moral confusion. Thirdly, it is merely representative of an immoral postmodern tendency in new Hollywood; and lastly *Blue Velvet* elicits moral confusion for the purposes of disputation. We have also established through these receptions that Lynch's agency fluctuates between the substantial to the ethereal in helping account for its meanings.

Let us now, though, take up this complicated theme of textual pleasure – which is for the most part sidestepped in the examples I cite above – through to this chapter's conclusion.

In 'Beyond the pleasure principle' Freud (1989: 600–5) observed that while the artist does not save the spectator 'the most painful experiences', those experiences 'can yet be felt by them as highly enjoyable' since 'under the dominance of the pleasure principle, there are ways and means enough of making what is in itself unpleasurable into a subject to be recollected and worked over in the mind'. The 'compulsion to repeat' the painful experience, moreover, is borne out of an 'instinct for mastery' that will 'lead to satisfaction'. The intimation for the example of *Blue Velvet* is that there is a shared but different sense of satisfaction for artist and theorist: Lynch will be working over an Oedipal trauma through his art, while the theorist's goal is to work over the unpleasurable disorder in the text in order to master it. But Freud, much like Barthes, was primarily interested in what lay beyond the pleasure principle; where the compulsion to repeat was still intrinsic (although not in Barthes's account), but where something, 'more primitive, more elementary, more instinctual than the pleasure principle' took hold.

In pursuing Freud's ideas we should pause momentarily to repeat his own observation that 'each of us is governed [...] by deep-rooted internal prejudices, into whose hands our speculation unwittingly plays' (1989: 624). Indeed, 'Beyond the pleasure principle' – the text through which he made public his thoughts on the ego/death instincts and the sexual/life instincts – is widely recognised as one of his most ambitious undertakings. Yet in citing Freud's ideas in lieu of the *evidence* supplied by the critical receptions of *Blue Velvet*, together with aspects of the text itself *and* details from the artist's biography, I believe that we are able to arrive at an outcome that offers some robust insights into the workings of artists, both in modern criticism, and in the public eye.

As we saw earlier, there was widespread conviction within the feminist reception of *Blue Velvet* that Lynch was consciously exploring Freudian concepts. And despite a strong disinclination towards declarations of principled causality, we can find in the fine detail of his biography that, when pushed on the topic, Lynch did grudgingly acknowledge as much ('it's all right there, yeah!' (Rodley 1997: 140)). If we follow the rationale that the text is our evidence of causality, then there is every reason to surmise (since we cannot know for certain from biographical accounts) that Lynch had familiarised himself with the detail of 'Beyond the pleasure principle' – and probably, by the other earlier accounts, 'Three essays on the theory of sexuality', 'The uncanny' and *The Interpretation of Dreams* too. But either way, this doesn't help us arrive at any dispassionate conclusions. In fact, if we are inclined to accept Lynch's stated method of working – in which daydreams 'are the ones that are important, the ones that come when I'm gently sitting in a chair letting my mind wander [while I] drive into a dream world that I've made or discovered; a world I choose' (Rodley 1997: 15) – then Lynch would seem to be artistically justified in his modernist intentions to allow his audience to experience (rather than master) the text he has produced. He is in the business, then, of producing the sorts or writerly texts Barthes preferred.

Returning to 'Beyond the pleasure principle', Freud proposed that a subject's libidinal instincts (these are other to our life instincts for self-preservation) operate within the ego and are determined historically within the 'pregenital organization' of a subject's development. And within this sexual instinct Freud identified the predominant 'presence of a sadistic component [that] can make itself independent and can, in the form of a perversion, dominate an individual's entire sexual activity'. For Freud, it was highly plausible that sadism was 'a death instinct which, under influence of the narcissism libido, has been forced away from the ego and to consequently only emerge in relation to the object [where] it now enters the service of a sexual function'. As he said,

> During the oral stage of organisation of the libido, the act of obtaining erotic mastery over an object coincides with that object's destruction. Later, the sadistic instinct separates off, and finally, at the stage of genital primacy, it takes on, for the purposes of reproduction, the function of overpowering the sexual object to the extent necessary for carrying out the sexual act. It

might indeed be said that the sadism which has been forced out of the ego has pointed the way for the libidinal components of the sexual instinct, and that these follow after it to the object. Whenever the original sadism has undergone no mitigation or intermixture, we find the familiar ambivalence of love and hate in erotic life [...] Masochism, the component instinct which is complementary to sadism, must [therefore] be regarded as sadism that has been turned round upon the subject's own ego. But there is no difference in principle between an instinct turning from an object to the ego and its turning from the ego to an object. (Freud 1989: 621)

There still seems little in Freud's observation to add any empirical outcomes to our existing discussions on *Blue Velvet*'s themes. It is one more variation competing on the themes of the film (despite its remarkable perceptiveness). But 'Beyond the pleasure principle' offers us the chance of a different set of outcomes if we are trying to learn more about the relationship between this text and its reception.

When we are talking about aesthetic pleasure in cases of postmodernism – where the conventions of high and popular culture comingle – then we are obliged to consider a fragmented audience. That is a distinction between the cultivated spectator who might place emphasis on film style, and the common spectator who privileges the film's plot. Indeed, while the film is recognised in the academic community as structurally ambiguous, this play on cinematic realism is executed by Lynch with a subtlety and aplomb that renders the film comprehensible if we are not paying close attention to these finer details. But under the pleasure principle, texts, if they are to 'have a yield of pleasure as their final outcome' and are unpleasurable in nature should, according to Freud 'be undertaken by some system of aesthetics with an economic approach' (1989: 601). Staiger (1992: 182), as well, noted in *Interpreting Films*, that 'what might count as an art film is quite different for each person but what makes the definition similar is their emphasis on the treatment of a very particular kind of subject matter. Art movies are no-holds-barred, frank; they are serious.' We have established, though, that the film accommodates a number of representational absurdities and anomalies that work against the graveness of the subject matter. In this respect the film appeared non-judgemental. And what is evident in our examples is that the cultured critic is inclined to bind any acknowledgment of 'guilty' pleasure to the film's stylistic bravura. In terms of *Blue Velvet*'s themes, meanwhile, mastery of the text is achieved by means of psychoanalytical (or Marxist) cipher codes. But what can we say now about principles of pleasure in relation to the film's public reception?

Freud (1989: 613) observed that the compulsion to repeat, exhibits a pronounced 'instinctual', or 'primaeval', character that, if acting in opposition to the bound pleasures of the pleasure principle – as the pregenital unbound ego/object instincts of masochism and sadism do – then the instinct gives 'the appearance of some "demonic" force at work' (as it does indeed in the primal scene). This instinct, moreover 'must be an old state of things, an initial state from which the living entity has at one time or other departed and to which it is striving to return by the circuitous paths along which its development leads' – a death drive towards an inanimate state.

In critical theory we find what might be seen under a Freudian analysis as 'an instinct towards perfection at work in human beings, which has brought them to their present high level of intellectual achievement and ethical sublimation [that] can easily be understood as a result of the instinctual repression upon which is based all that is most precious in human civilization'. In the examples I have offered here this intellectual achievement attaches itself to the ethical demands for sex and gender equities and, to a lesser extent, the class imbalances necessary to the advancements of capitalism. Such progression is, in fact, essential to our perception of societal development since 'the backward path that leads to complete satisfaction is a rule obstructed by the resistances which maintain the repression' (the repression in the field of critical theory being the author). Freud concluded, therefore, that 'there is no alternative but to advance in the direction in which growth is still free', although, as Freud observed, this growth comes 'with no prospect of bringing the process to a conclusion or of being able to reach a goal' (1989: 615).

But what of the backward public path – the path that Barthes suggested we travel – that might lead to 'complete satisfaction', or, bliss? In auteurist accounts, we may come back to Paisley Livingston's description (1997: 142) of an artistic 'type' (to which Lynch seems to belong) who exhibits a 'paradoxical modernist intention' whereby his films would appear to 'express his supreme indifference concerning the attitudes his work will make manifest'. But for Freud, the true artist 'understands how to work over his day-dreams in such a way as to make them lose what is too personal about them and repel strangers, and to make it possible for others to share in the enjoyment of them. He understands, too, how to tone them down so that they do not easily betray their origin from proscribed sources'. And when, Freud continued, the artist is, 'able to accomplish all this, he makes it possible for other people once more to derive consolation and alleviation from their own sources of pleasure in their unconscious which have become inaccessible to them' (1989: 423).

So we could say with *Blue Velvet* that Lynch was able to tap an unconscious source of collective pleasure that, according to *Monthly Film Bulletin*, earned its author the accolade of 'the most provocative and inspired director in the American mainstream' (Jenkins 1987), and was evidence that he had earned his audience's, 'gratitude and admiration' and had thus 'achieved *through* his phantasy what he had achieved only *in* his phantasy – honour,

Lynch and partner Isabella Rossellini, photographed by Helmut Newton.

power and the love of women' (Freud 1989: 423). And since perceptions of artistic standing are inextricably bound up with love and affection, hate and aggression – emotions that link us directly to 'the familiar ambivalence of love and hate in erotic life' – we can realistically conclude that we will no sooner do away with authors any more than we will do away with our instinctual desire for unbound pleasures, however much this hinders the judicious ideals that have underpinned the rejection of the author.

CHAPTER 5

Twin Peaks: The Rise and Fall of a Public Auteur

In pausing to take stock of our progress so far, we become aware of the fact that we have considered Lynch's cinematic influence within aesthetic expectations for generic works: the underground, or midnight movie, the Victorian period drama, the event picture and the auteur picture. Lynch offers us the opportunity now to explore wider spheres of authorial influence by taking into account institutional bearings on aesthetic receptions. Through his creative involvement with the television soap opera *Twin Peaks*, first broadcast (over two seasons) in the US between 1990 and 1991, Lynch's standing reached its apex. Indeed, if *Blue Velvet* was one of the cinematic events of its decade, then *Twin Peaks*, co-written and co-directed by Lynch (six of 29 episodes including the feature-length pilot), was to vie for a time as its television equal. For this brief moment in television history, Lynch was to command respect as an individual who had single-handedly refigured the conservative, ratings-led conventions of television soap opera. Indeed, in light of *Twin Peaks'* international success Lynch came to widespread public attention as something of an auteurist pioneer as both the popular and serious press rushed to eulogise Lynch as an author who had raised the seemingly artless glare of prime-time soap opera to new levels of credibility. Yet Lynch's continuing fascination with the secret life and death of *Twin Peaks'* homecoming queen, Laura Palmer, which took shape in the form of a movie prequel, *Twin Peaks: Fire Walk with Me* in 1992, was roundly viewed as an act of hubris; and of calculated commercial extortion. Seen subsequently as an artistic fraud, Lynch came to be damned by the critical press.

This chapter is for the most part, then, concerned with press criticism; by which we mean public criticism that is ostensibly non-partisan. In point of fact, all criticism is partisan to some degree, but journalistic critics need not be Lynch specialists, or fan-critics disposed to protect his reputation. In any case, the journalistic critic will be obliged to pass (relatively succinct) comment on texts whereas fans, biographers and academics will approach the authored text from a position of deductive reasoning. The suggestion here is not that journalistic receptions are somehow less germane. On the contrary, press criticism will reflect or set a yardstick for public opinion and tastes in a way that specialist writing will not. We will see at the conclusion of this chapter, in fact, that Lynch's biographers, amongst whom the feeling was that the film had been misrepresented, formed a collective challenge to the negative public reception of *Fire Walk with Me*, but, in doing so, merely fostered prejudices of a different kind.

Before we proceed, however, it is pertinent to acknowledge that a number of scholars sought to account for the cultural impact of the *Twin Peaks* phenomenon. In these treatises, the series tended to be viewed (rather perceptively as it has turned out) as indicative of a new wave in postmodern television. Scholarly interest in *Twin Peaks* was such that in 1993 *Film/Literature Quarterly* devoted a special issue 'Peaked Out!' (Lavery 1993) to the show while an anthology (also Lavery), *Full of Secrets: Critical Approaches to Twin Peaks*, appeared in 1994. In these and other commentaries (e.g. Ramsay 1991; Goldstein 1990) *Twin Peaks* drew praise and condemnation on a range of aesthetic, historical and ethical concerns, while Lynch's agency was an unshakable thesis running through these receptions. In his guest editorial for 'Peaked Out!', David Lavery (1993) set out the auteurist tone when he observed that it was through 'a prominent American director's first venture into television [that] complex and profound questions about the nature and function of television in the nineties' had been raised.

Henry Jenkins's study of 'fan critics' published in 1992, meanwhile, provided a perceptible example of how Lynch functioned in the show's reception amongst *Peaks* fans congregating in newly formed computer groups. Jenkins showed that an emphasis on authorship allowed male fans – who 'consistently appealed to knowledge about Lynch as an author as the central basis for their speculations about likely plot developments' – to defend their 'fascination with the soap opera-like dimensions of the series'. Jenkins (1992: 109–11) arrived at the view that:

> The fans' pleasure lay simultaneously in their textual mastery, their ability to predict the next twist of *Twin Peaks'* convoluted plot, and their vulnerability to Lynch's trickery, their inability to guess what is likely to happen next [...] Their pleasure in speculating about narrative enigmas, thus, depended upon the presence of a powerful author whose hand orders events and bestows significance.

Twin Peaks: The Rise of the Television Auteur

Any number of film histories map technological and artistic struggles between television and cinema. Cinema's economic need to distinguish itself from television by means of new technologies has helped film historians delineate periods of new Hollywood. At various historical junctures sound, colour, widescreens, digital technologies and so on have all contributed to the specialness of the 'night out' at the movies. At the same time, the politique had bestowed the auteur upon the cinema and in doing so offered it a lasting institutional respectability. Through the creative interventions of special directors like Lynch, cinema – unlike television – became a medium that could stretch the processed edges of popular entertainment and might even engage a more discerning audience. As a medium for creative expression, then, commercial television has endured a critical history as cinema's poor relation, since it has generally been perceived as an artless medium at the fundamental service of commerce (through advertising). For this reason, press accounts tended to view Lynch's associations with the *Twin Peaks* project as wholly atypical.

In its critical outlook, this chapter is engaged principally with issues of poetic novelty and institutions. Like cinema, literature accommodates both generic and poetic fictions while the learned critic helps us distinguish between the two. Yet on an institutional level, prime-time American television has been thought of historically as a populist medium that is hostile to poetic indulgence. Brad Chisholm illustrates this point in his essay 'Difficult viewing: the pleasure of complex screen narratives', in which he offers a précis of phenomenological accounts of the medium. Chisholm reminds his reader that television provides 'an escape from thought', and that it 'numbs the mind' (Waterson), that it is 'a long term menace to reason' (Maynard), an 'escape from the cognitive body' (Nelson) as well as 'a social and aesthetic pariah' (Chisholm 1991). Institutional prejudice such as this, we will find, underscored the majority of journalistic articles that tried to make sense of *Twin Peaks*.

Given this institutional prejudice, it is perhaps not surprising that the auteur has been an undistinguished figure in the promotion and reception of popular television (even if one immediately thinks of *Alfred Hitchcock Presents* as a most apparent exception to this rule). Certainly, American network television was not the place critics expected to come across an auteur. In his article published in *The New Yorker* on the eve of *Twin Peaks*' network premier, for instance, Terrence Rafferty (1990a) thought the idea of Lynch 'creating a series for network television' sounded 'like a joke', since his films were (although he was to revise this view) 'everything that American television isn't: adventurous, disturbing, erotic, visually exciting and absolutely personal'. Much to Rafferty's surprise, however, Lynch had approached television drama 'with an imaginative intensity' that had made 'it strange and new'. It was as if, he surmised, Lynch hadn't been able to distinguish 'between the highest movie art and the lowest television craft'. So what, we are destined to ask, were the textual and industrial confluences that in 1990 saw the critical industries celebrate *Twin Peaks* as a television event?

In beginning to address this question I want to draw upon Jauss's ideas on the 'individual text' and the text's intertextual relationships that become 'formative of a genre' (Jauss 1982: 87). As we have established, horizons of expectation accord with the reader's understandings of the conventions to which the new text relates. *Twin Peaks* caught the imagination in such a way that horizons of expectation for prime-time television drama were altered. We will return to this point, but first I want to ascertain the specificity, as the critical industries saw it, of *Twin Peaks* as a generic 'masterwork': a text that is definable by Jauss in terms of its 'formal ossification, automatization, or a giving-up or misunderstanding of the "rules of the game"' (Jauss 1982: 94).

Selling *Twin Peaks*

The rise of the auteur picture during the period of post-classicism represents a film industry that had learned to adapt to niche markets. The auteur is, therefore, no longer only an anonymous figure whose autograph is waiting there to be discovered by the critic. With Hollywood's increased emphasis on marketing, the signature of the auteur becomes all-important in the promotion of their films. I have made the point already, but we might bring to mind once more the fact that 'A Film by David Lynch', elicits its own horizons of expectations on both a personal and a generic level. Even so, despite being read very much as a Lynchian text, *Twin Peaks* was not marketed on Lynch's name. It became incumbent upon the critical industries to identify, and subsequently eulogise, Lynch as *Twin Peaks'* creative mastermind; and it was Lynch who accounted for *Twin Peaks'* elements of novelty.

While most critics took up *Twin Peaks* as a Lynch text, the series was the most collaborative enterprise that Lynch had taken, or been given, creative credit for. Hughes provides a detailed breakdown of Lynch's input on the series and lists 14 separate directors and a total of eight writers (with Lynch credited only as the series' co-creator and as co-writer and director of the pilot, and episodes 2, 8, 9, 14 and 29 of the series' 29 shows). Indeed, by the time ABC gave the go-ahead for the second series, Lynch was fulfilling work commitments on his fifth feature, *Wild at Heart*. This detail was not lost on *Twin Peaks'* co-creator Mark Frost who, in referring to the series' reception, remarked that 'there were times when David [Lynch] was making *Wild at Heart*, when I was doing almost *all* the work on *Twin Peaks'*. But, as Frost rued 'everybody want[ed] to believe in the auteur theory, that it all somehow springs from one person, and David [Lynch] had [the] much higher profile' (Hughes 2002: 104–38).

Unlike his cinematic works, however, Lynch's name features only after the cast list, firstly as 'created by Mark Frost and David Lynch' and then as co-writer and as director of the episodes he worked on directly in these capacities. In consolidating the point that Lynch's agency was superfluous to marketing needs, we might also refer to a full-page advertisement for *Twin Peaks* that appeared in *The New York Times* on the day of the pilot's US television premiere. This advertisement paraded the show's quality by employing a convention of cinematic marketing that assembles an arrangement of stirring critical notices:

Time, October 1990.

'"Twin Peaks" – the series that will change TV';

'"Twin Peaks" … like nothing else on television';

'the most hauntingly original work ever done for American TV';

'"Twin Peaks" will change television history'[1] and so on.

Although this advertisement omitted authorial origins, it nevertheless carried the promise of a quality television drama. But we must not let this obscure the fact that *Twin Peaks* was also sold on its more populist and humorous attributes (albeit after the show had already made its reputation). Taking the jacket for the *Twin Peaks* videocassette collection, for instance, we find that rather than call attention to Lynch's name (it is, in fact, absent) the jacket promotes images of the cast (Sheryl Lee/Laura Palmer and Kyle MacLachlan/Special Agent Cooper) and combines these with Cooper's comedic catchphrase 'damn fine'. Additionally, the jacket promises 'Over 2 hours of Damn Fine Viewing' and a '"Damn Fine" Promotion' where fans can order merchandise such as enamel logo badges and T-shirts ('in moody black') that carried a 'wacky' *Twin Peaks* caption. There was also opportunity for fans to enter a competition with 'Damn Fine Prizes to be Won' including an 'all expenses paid trip for two to the homeland of *Twin Peaks*'.[2] Signifiers such as these do not, as a rule, carry the pledge of an auteurist text.

New Textual Horizons

In the reception of new texts the critic will firstly institute appropriate horizons against which that text will be measured. And it is 'in the artistic creation', as Bazin put it in his famous essay 'La politique des auteurs' (1981: 45), that 'the personal factor [acts] as a criterion of reference' which then 'continues and even progresses from one film to the next'. This is not to say, of course, that the generic work does not also act as a reference for departure (as we will see shortly). But the fact that Lynch, by now a bona-fide auteur, had hopped institutional enclosures – had embraced, moreover, such a gratuitously corporate institution – dismayed many critics. Rafferty, indeed, asked (1990a) 'what could he [Lynch] possibly do for the bland, timid corporate medium of prime-time television? And what could it do for him (other than make studio moviemaking look liberating by comparison)?'. It was not, though, that Lynch's films were completely ignored as points of reference (the small-town milieus of *Blue Velvet* and *Twin Peaks* acted as the most common textual association), rather that the presence of a poetic text, and the incumbent artist per se, flouted expectations for a prime-time television drama.

Given that authorial intertexts were not the name of the game here, the tendency of the critic was to think of *Twin Peaks* generically and to identify the generic paradigms from which the show departed. In this context, *Dallas*, the durable prime-time American soap (running for some 14 seasons between 1978 and 1991) frequently offered the critic said expectations.

Dramatic events in the small-town (the series' opening credit sequence featured a roadside notice that declared 'welcome to *Twin Peaks*, population 51,201') woodland setting of *Twin Peaks* were initiated by the discovery of the dead body of the seemingly upright, all-American, prom queen, Laura Palmer. 'Who killed Laura Palmer?' became the central enigma with the series' chief protagonist, FBI Special Agent Dale Cooper (MacLachlan), sent into the community to assist local Sheriff, Harry S. Truman (Michael Ontkean), with the investigation into Laura's death. The *Twin Peaks* Press Kit had promised a series in which 'no one is quite what they appear to be and almost everyone has something to hide'; a series, it continued, where 'Cooper and Truman's probe into Laura's death uncovers many busy secrets in Twin Peaks'. Indeed, the Press Kit set out the series' enigmas thus:

> Was Laura leading a sordid double existence?
> Did she find out that her erstwhile boyfriend, Bobby Briggs, was having an affair with a married woman?
> Why would well-respected businessmen scheme to take over the valuable Packard sawmill property?
> Why is Catherine Martell so bitterly jealous of her brother's widow, the beautiful and imperious mill owner Jocelyn Packard?

This teasing synopsis was supported with the promise of a luscious melodrama as 'each revelation lays bare whole other worlds, as we delve deeper and deeper into the characters' fantasies, loves and obsessions' (Twin Peaks Press Kit, www.twinpeaks.org/archives/press). In thematic respect (broadly the revelation of characters' secrets and closet skeletons, the dealings and double-crossings and in its general binaries of honesty and corruption), *Dallas*, the familial melodrama of feuding oil magnates, worked for the critic as a kind of generic template for *Twin Peaks*. Indeed, the tag line 'who killed Laura Palmer?' was discussed on more than one occasion as a direct reference to *Dallas*' own lingering enigma – 'who shot J.R.?' – that had so caught the public zeitgeist a little over a decade earlier.

The prime-time exhibition slots of the two shows, with the first season (12 April–23 May 1990) of *Twin Peaks* broadcast by ABC on Thursdays between 9 and 10 pm and of *Dallas* (between 1979 and 1991) by CBS on Fridays at the same time, is of equal significance. Still, in terms of the popularity of the two shows, comparisons between them need to be understood relatively. While viewing figures do not take account of shifting audience demographics, on its opening (and highest rated) show *Twin Peaks* attracted 35 million viewers (a mere 33 per cent of the overall viewing figures in the US (Bremner 1990), compared to the 41,470,000 (a 76 per cent share and the second highest viewing figures for a single episode in American television history) *Dallas* achieved in November 1980 when J.R. Ewing's would-be assassin was revealed (www.dallas. tvtome.com).

For all the thematic and scheduling consistencies between *Twin Peaks* and *Dallas* (or for that matter other contemporary prime-time TV serial dramas such as *Dynasty* and *The Colbys*), the former marked its difference as a text in quite particular poetic terms. It would serve us no purpose to systematically delineate those differences, but brief reference to Chisholm's detailed structural breakdown of the two shows is helpful here in understanding the nature of *Twin Peaks* as a generic masterwork. Speaking of *Twin Peaks* in terms of its 'narrative difficulty', Chisholm (1991) showed that while *Dallas* utilised no more than three to five plot lines in any given episode, *Twin Peaks* featured up to 11. He stressed the fact that as the series developed, the primary enigma of who killed Laura Palmer became 'supplemented with numerous other mysteries that appeared unrelated' while at the same time 'sub-mysteries seemed to be forgotten for weeks'. 'Nearly every week' he continued 'an additional plot line was introduced, yet one was resolved (or forsaken) only every fourth or fifth episode'.

The series marked its difference in other ways too. Chisholm refers to *Twin Peaks*' 'unusual canons of probability' that manifest visually in examples such as an 'inexplicable' ceiling-high '"sculpture" of office furniture' and the story of the '39-year-old eye patch-touting Nadine' who (having acquired the strength of 10 men following an accident) joins the high school wrestling team (1991). *Variety*, meanwhile, picked out compositional differences between the two shows and reported that, in contrast to the 'polish and gloss' of *Dallas*, *Twin Peaks* went against 'the staples of TV grammar' by 'holding shots too long, indulging in slow dissolves and extreme close-ups' and 'isolating telling images' (Guider 1990). We can recall that Staiger (1992: 46) argued that Jauss's emphasis on aesthetic horizons had been to the 'practical neglect of discursive, social, political and economic contexts'. But in its make up as poetic prime-time soap, *Twin Peaks* was something of an anomaly; a plural text that confused the social and institutional realms to which Staiger's argument initially applied.

A number of essayists have described the historical and industrial contexts that gave rise to a series such as *Twin Peaks*. As I have indicated already, the common thread running through these receptions is the concept of postmodernism and *Twin Peaks* is often viewed as an exemplary postmodern text and not just, as Jim Collins (1993: 767–71) had it, because the series 'involved David Lynch a bona fide postmodernist filmmaker'. Indeed, Collins's account offers a concise, although in my view overstated, reminder of how *Twin Peaks* 'as would-be cinema and would-be soap opera', came to represent 'a fundamental change in the way the entertainment industries' had come to 'envision their publics' and marked a point at which television recognised that modern audiences are culturally strewn, or, to use Collins's term 'microcultural'. Collins spoke of *Twin Peaks* bringing together 'interlocking appeals' and in asking its audience to 'negotiate [an] array of signs and subject positions', the series had helped 'redefine the nature of entertainment in contemporary cultures'.

But for all its 'microcultural' appeals, Collins maintained that *Twin Peaks* communicated primarily to a cultural elite (the show's wider audience having quickly tired of its structural novelty). Collins rationalises his claim with reference to the impact of new technologies – the videocassette recorder and cable television particularly – that offered, for those who could afford it at that time, many more viewing alternatives to the 'big three' network channels. *Time Magazine* carried an article that lent support to this argument with Richard Zoglin (1990) putting the case that the success of a 'difficult' show such as *Twin Peaks* was 'testimony to changing times in network television'. In a decade where network channels were attracting only two-thirds of the 90 per cent of the audience figures they commanded during the 1980s, Zoglin believed that 'a show of limited appeal like *Twin Peaks* can make it' since the 'art-house audience' had 'become a marketing niche'. Indeed, as Collins (1993: 342) reminded us, this was the era of the affluent, educated and materialistic city dweller – the 'yuppie' – and it was the acquaintance of the 'yuppie', so Collins believed, that advertisers wanted to buy through *Twin Peaks*' advertising windows.

Receiving *Twin Peaks* as a Poetic Text

It is marketing's job to exploit horizontal expectations of one sort or another, and while *Twin Peaks* was not publicly marketed on Lynch's name, the *Twin Peaks* press kit did instruct journalists that 'world renowned director David Lynch [had brought] his incomparable visual artistry to "Twin Peaks", a disturbing mystery about the seemingly typical small town' (Twin Peaks Press Kit). We can do no more than guess at the direct influence of the press kit on journalistic interpretations of *Twin Peaks*. All the same, we know it was Lynch's (rather than co-creator Mark Frost's) name that helped account for the show's innovation (at least until the *Twin Peaks* hyperbole settled) with the effect that auteurism – which, like all paradigms 'presupposes something provisionally to be understood' (Jauss 1982: 140) – more generally became a fashionable critical paradigm for television reviewing. The older generic paradigm, in other words, was unable to manage this new masterwork, with the effect that meaning now privileged the individual over the generic.

The tendency amongst serious journalists was to write Lynch's move into television in near prophetic terms. Collins makes this point in his discussion on the reception of *Twin Peaks* in the US. Yet in my view, it seems that Collins too hastily passed over the fact that *Twin Peaks* became a pan-national television event, which, despite its auteurist receptions, was not pitched solely at a culturally refined audience. In the run up to *Twin Peaks*' US opening *Variety*, in fact, carried a report on ABC's 'in house research' that showed that the series, which according to Frost 'adhere[d] to the classical serial formula and detective conventions' but to which he and Lynch had brought 'a twist', appealed to 'two distinct groups of viewers: younger, hipper audiences who probably liked Lynch's feature film "Blue Velvet" and probably watch shows like "thirtysomething" and "Late Night with David Letterman" and more traditional viewers who regularly watch daytime or evening soaps' (Guider 1990).

This is a point we will take forward now, on the grounds that the widespread circulation of Lynch's name – mostly through associations with *Twin Peaks*

– contributed to Lynch's celebrity and extended expansive perceptions of his poetic signature into public territory. In tracing these ideas we will now focus particularly on *Twin Peaks*' reception in the British press.

While *Broadcast* magazine reported on the 'terrible deluge of hype' (Day-Lewis 1990) that had repelled some sections of the media, the British press had waited in puzzled anticipation as word crossed the Atlantic that *Twin Peaks* mania was sweeping America. The pilot episode had, in fact, appeared in Europe as a freestanding feature on video rental a year earlier. While the release of the video passed with little notice, the broadsheet press had picked up on a new work from Lynch. Sheila Johnson (1989) writing in *The Independent* offered a single paragraph review that reported that the BBC had acquired the series for broadcast a year on and that 'Lynch's off-key direction and bizarre ten minute coda' (reference to the freestanding pilot's imposed ending) 'slides a long, long, way from tele-realism into screen territory that is very odd indeed'. But by the time of the show's first episode, broadcast on 23 October 1990, countless articles had appeared in the tabloid and broadsheet press.

In one article, *Today* carried the headline 'The wacky soap you have to quote to prove that you are not a philistine', and advised that 'the only clue to [*Twin Peaks*'] surreal puzzle is the fact that avant-garde British (sic) filmmaker David Lynch directs and co-writes the show' (Middlehurst 1990). In another *Today* article entitled 'Lynch's peak of perfection', Sue Heal (1990) singled out Lynch for individual praise for 'bravely taking up the challenge of working within a new medium unhampered by the famous rule book', while *The Sunday Express* told its readers that it was 'Time to get clued up on Peakspeak' and praised 'television's latest blockbuster [...] filmed by cult director David Lynch' for the way it 'manipulates the viewers [through] the brilliant mixing of comedy, tragedy and even farce' (Russell 1990).

The Mail on Sunday, meanwhile, carried a double-page spread entitled 'Are you ready for Twin Peaks?' in which readers was forewarned that 'TV would never be the same again', and in describing Lynch as 'surreal', accordingly drew attention to the show's enigmatic and hard to believe qualities: 'whose bacon is cremated? What is the secret of the one eyed woman?' and who is 'Waldo the eye-witness mynah bird?' (Purgavie 1990). There were a total of three fictional tie-in books, *The Autobiography of FBI Special Agent Dale Cooper: My Life, My Times*, *Welcome to Twin Peaks* and *The Secret Diary of Laura Palmer*, all published between 1990/91. The

Mail on Sunday even carried the 'exclusive serialisation' of *The Secret Diary of Laura Palmer* – written by, or to be absolutely accurate 'as seen by', Jennifer Lynch (Lynch's daughter). The paper introduced the serialisation with a 'Four-page special on a Cult Phenomenon', that promised to reveal 'the missing clues to TV's most mysterious whodunit' and promised lurid extra-textual insights into the 'tortured mind of a brilliant student who hid the dark mystery of her death' (Lynch 1990).

In the broadsheet press the auteurist bent was, as expected, rather more emphatic. Writing for *The Independent*, Reggie Nadelson (1990) suggested that Lynch, who 'had never done TV' – because 'he is an artist' – had with *Twin Peaks* produced 'the first masterpiece of the Nineties'. Ian Penman (1990) writing in *The Sunday Correspondent* joined in the applause arguing that although Lynch only directed two of the shows, *Twin Peaks* 'bears his signature through and through'. 'With a residue of prickly surrealism in his heart', he continued 'Lynch is rethinking the surface of American life'. In *The Times*, meanwhile, Charles Bremner (1990) reported that although British audiences were more familiar with the 'offbeat' coexisting with the 'commonplace' (British audiences might have more plastic horizons of expectation than their American counterparts, having been reared on BBC (public service) television that produced surreal shows such as *The Singing Detective* and *Monty Python's Flying Circus*) in America, *Twin Peaks* was being hailed as 'a cultural turning point'. Bremner argued, indeed, that Lynch could be credited with instigating 'one of the most ambitious experiments so far by one of the old [American] networks'. By the time the show was first broadcast in the UK, Lynch's standing was such that one of the UK's leading cultural commentators, Mark Lawson (1990) for *The Independent on Sunday*, was to report that 'a messianic apparatus had been erected around Lynch' and his 'upmarket mini-series'. Indeed, on *Twin Peaks*' blanket appeal Lawson remarked,

> In Britain … it has been said for years that the shared cultural experience (everyone talking about the same programme on the morning after) is dead because of the proliferating channels and video rentals, but people were talking about *Twin Peaks* on the morning before and after across the whole newspaper market, with the warmest praise coming from *The Sun*.

However, the early enthusiasm in Britain for *Twin Peaks*' novelty was quick to diminish; the show's waning critical and commercial fortunes mirroring the pattern already set in the US. In an article carried following the final episode of the first series in the UK, *The Independent* reported that *Twin Peaks'* second season had ultimately languished at number 87 in the top 100 US ratings list 'a descent mirrored in miniature by its UK outing: BARB record[ing] a slump from four million plus viewers to two million' (Lyttle 1991). The tabloids, in fact, had begun to tire of the show as early as the second episode of the first series with *The Daily Mail* commenting that *Twin Peaks* was 'all style and no substance and would probably only have the tiniest audience were it not for all the hype' (Paterson 1990). In London's *Evening Standard* Victoria Mather (1990) complained that Lynch 'didn't care if anybody watched it or not' on the grounds that 'dwarfs who talk backwards was his own private joke' while by the third episode Pam Francis (1990), writing in *Today*, was asking 'who cares about Laura Palmer?' since she 'sounded like a nasty piece of work' and a character for whom she had 'lost … sympathy'. By the end of series one, meanwhile, *The Sun* had, like the show's Sheriff Truman 'had enough' of 'the dreams, the dwarfs, the giants, Tibet and the rest of the hocus-pocus', and 'of the series *Twin Peaks*' (Cunningham 1991) as a whole.

The interest in the broadsheets was also on the wane, with *The Independent* left to wonder how it was that 'something so banal as who killed Laura Palmer could have "obsessed" a nation?' (Lyttle 1991). Nevertheless, there remained a tangible feeling of respect for Lynch's achievements. In another article, the same paper attributed the show's demise in quality to the idea that Lynch had handed 'virtually all scripts and direction to pupils' with the result that the show had become 'more and more recognisably, School Of Lynch' and it was 'only rarely that a convincing copy [was] achieved' ('Twin Peaks' 1991). In *The Times* Patrick Stoddard (1990) echoed these sentiments, writing that 'if the remarkable David Lynch had directed all seven episodes himself, things might have turned out differently, but what we got for five of them was other directors forlornly trying to think themselves into Lynch's head'. And Stoddard continued that had he begun his article with '"Now is the winter of our discontent" [he] would not, on balance, fool many people into thinking [he] was Shakespeare'. Lyttle (1991) surmised, finally, that for all its shortcomings, one should not 'lose sight of *Twin Peaks'* achievements', since it 'had brought blood, eroticism and a liberating craziness to squeaky clean American primetime'.

Twin Peaks and Cinematic Horizons

So far we have seen how the poetic text was warmly (if fleetingly) welcomed as a new horizon for prime-time television drama. As the Lynchian effect has showed us, US popular television could now respectfully accommodate the auteur. There are, though, interesting institutional prejudices to be observed if we turn now to a conjunctural analysis of the reception of *Twin Peaks*, *Wild at Heart* and *Twin Peaks: Fire Walk with Me*.

As we know, the auteur picture will knowingly restyle or work against the conventions of a given genre or genres. Yet in the public reception of the American art picture the general feeling remains amongst critics that commercial cinema is a rudimentarily populist form that must yield only so much in terms of artistic self-expression. And, of course, the American art picture is itself recognisable through its own set of conventions. Both David Bordwell and Steve Neale have accounted for the aesthetic shape of the postwar art film. Bordwell (1999: 716) has argued that American art cinema is the descendent of earlier European art cinemas and certain modernist literature. He also argued, however, that the 'more radical avant-garde movements, such as Soviet montage filmmaking, Surrealism, and *cinéma pur* seem to have been relatively without effect upon art cinema style', since, so Bordwell suspects 'those experimental styles which did not fundamentally change narrative coherence were the most assimilating to the postwar art cinema'. Neale (1976), meanwhile, spoke of New Hollywood in terms of its package systems that are 'geared precisely to finance-capital interests' and the proliferation of the 'relatively cheaper techniques' associated historically with the New Wave and ciné-vérité movements. Yet these descriptions are not altogether typical of Lynch's films. With this in mind, I want to turn to the issues of generic authorship in its specific relationship to the reception of *Wild at Heart* (1990) and the *Twin Peaks* texts (that is television and filmic) since these works circulated at the same historical moment.

One of the central tenets of Jauss's reception model is the conviction that variances in interpretation cannot be solely accounted for through differences in personality. Indeed, the fact that Jauss's proposition pictures a paradigmatic reader might be thought of as the horizon model's Achilles' heel in the sense that it controls the potential for the reader to write individual meanings into the text. Even so, the auteurist's preference for originality and genius; the division between the generic and the unique, is a preference nurtured under a capitalist paradigm since it acts to extol the merits of individualism. Such a proposal is diametric to the medieval paradigm that Jauss identifies and in which the generic masterwork – 'definable in terms of the alteration of the horizon of the genre that is as unexpected as it is enriching' (1982: 94) – was welcomed for the aesthetic opportunities it opened up. If we follow Jauss's direction we can say, in empirical terms if nothing else, that the artist only serves market needs in the sense that the auteurist text and the generic masterwork remain one and the same thing.

I have demonstrated already (in my discussion of *Dune*) that generic analysis is compelled to consider the point at which a given genre stops and another takes over. In the public domain, though, generic borders are rather more happily assumed. And as we have seen elsewhere, the functional role of generic categories is to serve the broadest organisational demands of a film's production, promotion and reception. This is true of the auteur picture too, where the tendency of the critic is to automatically sub-divide the post-classical art picture such as *Wild at Heart* and *Twin Peaks: Fire Walk with Me* into sub-generic (Lynchian/auteurist) categories. That is, there exist horizontal expectations for an auteur picture and horizontal expectations for a Lynch picture. Although these two domains will never be truly independent of one another, it is on the critics' understanding of conventions in both domains that the auteurist work comes to be judged. Lynch, like other auteurs, is praised as an individual, but an individual kept in check by what is deemed permissible within cinematic limits.

Lynch's affection for lapsed-causal narrations – most unmistakable in films such as *Twin Peaks: Fire Walk with Me*, *Lost Highway* and *INLAND EMPIRE* – might be offered (even in line with Lynch's other films) as an indication of the variable structural scales of post-classical art cinema. Still, the critical reception of *Wild at Heart* and *Twin Peaks: Fire Walk with Me* shows that in the early 1990s, auteurist critics were less than tolerant of Lynch's structural experimentation within the institutional jurisdiction of commercial American art cinema (although in the next chapter we shall see that this proposition becomes rather more complicated).

The auteurist readings of *Twin Peaks* (through Lynch) were not formed in the same way as the reading of Lynch's cinematic texts. Examples I have provided elsewhere in this book show how auteurist accounts of, say, *Blue Velvet* and *Dune*, sought out a Lynchian worldview and/or mise en scène (or lack of it) in very insistent ways. In the public reception of *Twin Peaks* it was usually enough to identify Lynch as an avant-garde or a surrealist (even 'weird' in many cases) filmmaker. The novelty was that a poetic text had plotted a route into a new and unexpected institutional arena. The release of *Wild at Heart* (on 17 August 1990 in the US and a week later in the UK) roughly punctuated the broadcast of the first series of *Twin Peaks* on either side of the Atlantic yet readings of the two texts overlapped only superficially. Reviews of *Twin Peaks* vis-à-vis *Wild at Heart*, in other words, may have acknowledged Lynch as an authorial common denominator but more comprehensive intertextual associations were atypical. *Wild at Heart* was, after all, recognised as a violently kinetic road movie and so didn't obviously attract associations with the lazy televisual milieu of the *Twin Peaks* American/Canadian border town.

Wild at Heart, Lynch's adaptation of Barry Gifford's book of the same name, starred Nicolas Cage (Sailor Ripley) and Laura Dern (Lula) as lovers fleeing hired assassins across America. But despite the fact that the *Wild at Heart* was awarded the prestigious Palme d'Or prize at the 1990 Cannes Film Festival, and, moreover, a promotional campaign that promised, amongst

Dern and Cage in *Wild at Heart*.

other cinematic treats, a 'Bonfire of a movie that confirms David Lynch as the most exciting and innovative filmmaker of his generation,'[3] the critical tide had begun to turn against Lynch.

By the time of *Wild at Heart*'s release, critics had a clear sense of what a Lynch film should be. Anne Billson (1990), for instance, describing Lynch as 'the king of weirdness' thought his films should be 'arty and strange and packed with banal non-sequiturs' while Margaret Walters (1990) suggested that 'a David Lynch film [was] expected to be startling and brazenly peculiar'. But although a Lynch text could still be recognisably Lynchian, critics began to make more general demands that Lynch the auteur be innovative. With *Wild at Heart* Walters warned that Lynch 'was in danger of repeating himself, of watering down his originality [...] by playing to [his] audience[s'] expectations'.

It would be misleading to suggest that with *Wild at Heart* Lynch was roundly written off on grounds of an innovatory lack. For instance, and although not altogether enamoured with the film, Anthony Lane (1990) felt that Lynch's strength was still evident in his 'fresh [...] vision of dire conspiracies' while Hilary Mantel (1990) thought that the film's 'first hour has touches of brilliance and deft changes in pace and tone'. However, a number of reviews detected derivative processes at work. Rafferty (1990), who in his glowing review of *Twin Peaks*, we might recall, suggested that Lynch's films were 'the highest movie art', described *Wild at Heart* as 'inexpressive and trivial, even silly'. Chris Sharrett (1991), meanwhile, wondered if 'there was *ever* anything genuinely provocative (much less progressive) to his [Lynch's] work in the first place', and in his review entitled 'Artificial heart', Alexander Walker (1990) warned that with this 'overwrought and over hyped' film 'Lynch's audience may find him out'. 'He isn't really an American visionary', he concluded, 'maybe he [Lynch] had a dream at one time' but with *Wild at Heart* 'it has turned into a formula'.

To find a formula is to suggest that the experiment is done with. Yet if we contrast these assessments with Lynch's next cinematic venture, *Twin Peaks: Fire Walk with Me*, we can identify a number of contradictions at play with regard to accepted levels of cinematic expression. On the one hand, by making a movie prequel of the *Twin Peaks* television series Lynch courted charges of repetition and calculated aesthetic extortion. On the other, more general expectations of Lynch as an auteur and what was perceived as cinematically permissible were at issue.

Most critics found *Twin Peaks: Fire Walk with Me* difficult to comprehend and/or distasteful. The film – co-scripted with Robert Engels[4] (rather than Frost who acted on this project in the capacity of Executive Producer) – was the first of a three-picture deal (in the event it was only two due to legal complications) struck between Lynch and the European production company CIBY-2000. CIBY-2000 afforded Lynch his usual demands for creative freedoms while he also enjoyed new creative opportunities opened up by an 18-certificate rating (both *Blue Velvet* and *Wild at Heart* were rated 18 in the UK). The series began with the discovery of Laura Palmer's corpse while the film traced the seven days leading up to her death. But, whereas the television series only implied and imagined the sordid detail of Lara Palmer's life, the film was a much darker and more graphic affair that addressed the thematic taboos of incest and filicide in much more pronounced and ambiguous ways.

Assessments of *Twin Peaks: Fire Walk with Me* frequently made reference to the fact that the film was denounced at its 1992 Cannes Film Festival premier. Indeed, Scott Murray (1992) reported in his transcript of the *Twin Peaks: Fire Walk with Me* Press Conference (at Cannes) that Lynch's entrance to the conference room was 'to the accompaniment of hissing and booing'. But what was it that critics found so distasteful about the film? And what might this tell us about our horizons of expectation for cinematic artworks and their authors?

A number of critics objected to the film because Lynch seemed to treat with contempt the very spirit of cinematic artistry. *Twin Peaks: Fire Walk with Me* amounted to a calculated act of commercial exploitation it was felt. Murray, for instance, asked if Lynch's continued investment in the *Twin Peaks* project represented 'a lack of inspiration' or had he (Lynch) just 'wanted some kind of time-out?'. Desmond Christy (1992) reported that the film was 'neither a masterpiece nor a film (sic) [but the] somewhat sad result of a typical business conversation between inexperienced (European) producers and a fame-hungry (American) director' while Nigel Andrews (1992), who, having described Lynch previously as a genius, argued that he had become 'the most annoying director in America' and wondered if *Fire Walk with Me* was 'the exhausted ravings of a writer-director still trying to coax money from a cult TV series?'. Geoff Andrew (2000), finally, thought that the film 'looked like off-cuts from the series that were eliminated because they were either too nasty or too inept; and that the film's producers had made 'no attempt to conceal the cynicism that presumably motivated their desire to cash in on their TV success'. (The besmirched relationship between the artist and the market is one I will pursue more purposely through my discussion of Lynch's television advertisements in the following chapter.)

Other critics turned on Lynch because the film's level of formal experimentation – its 'artistic doodlings' and 'unique conceptual sequences' as *Variety* (McCarthy 1992) succinctly put it – was perceived to be too distracting for mainstream audiences. So, while some critics saw the film as commercial extortion, others thought that Lynch had contravened the rules of comprehension for commercial cinema. Sheridan Morley (1992) asked 'who cares who killed Laura Palmer?' and protested that although a 'Canadian border may be boring […] that [was] no reason to inflict this hallucinatory mishmash on any but the most die-hard fan'. 'Nothing', he continued, could 'justify the money spent' on a film with such 'stunning disregard for audience values'. Alexander Walker (1992) expressed similar sentiments when suggesting that 'the whole production exudes a contempt for viewers' and that the film's 'deconstruction of the narrative' was an 'incoherent [and] tedious experience'. Geoff Brown (1992) remarked that 'with no linear plot…jolting visions and bizarre encounters' the film would 'alienate all comers' while for Sue Heal (1992), *Fire Walk with Me* 'was akin to having [her] brain slowly spit-roasted on a barbecue until all its working parts have been blacked to a crisp'. Inevitably (in press accounts anyway) Lynch's own reputation as an auteur had reached its nadir. Iain Johnstone (1992) thought that 'the decidedly dodgy talents of David Lynch' had 'lurch[ed] into an incoherent ramble'. But that 'need not concern anybody interested in satisfying cinema' since Lynch had displayed 'arrogance in thinking that his private hallucinations [could] make public entertainment'. Harry Pearson (1992) concurred, suggesting that *Twin Peaks: Fire Walk with Me* was:

> So bad that it virtually forces us to re-assess the entire output of the man and to wonder how so many of us could have been so wrong (and for so long) about Lynch's cinematic skills. At 134 minutes, the senseless glimpse into a kind of kooky, snide, cheesy milieu which could exist neither on this nor any other planet seems as if it will never end.

On the evidence of the negative reception of *Twin Peaks: Fire Walk with Me*, we find that the journalistic critic will see it as a requirement of the true auteur to rise above commercial obligations, while remaining respectful of their audience (on whose behalf the critic assumes to speak). Although these same prejudices also exist in the book-length surveys of Lynch's work, dedicated biographical books will tend to be auteurist sponsors and will serve thus as strategic builders and protectors of artistic legends. In their reassessments of *Fire Walk with Me*, not one of Lynch's biographers entertained accusations of 'cashing in' on the television show's popularity. In fact quite the opposite was true, with these sources showing a pattern that *reclaimed the film* as something of a misunderstood (albeit potentially flawed) work of cinematic art. In these evaluations, Lynch's structural experimentation did not read as a forlorn 'disregard for audience values' at all; on the contrary, *Fire Walk with Me* was viewed rather, in the words of Hughes (2002: 182), as 'an overlooked cinematic masterpiece'. Nochimson (1997: 173), indeed, suggested that the film had been 'misconstrued' and championed its 'daring and its singularity', Chion (1996: 159) maintained that although the film was 'unbalanced [...] an opera without a finale', *Fire Walk with Me* 'contained some of contemporary cinema's strongest scenes' and had brought cinema 'back to its variegated wealth', while Rodley (1997: 156) spoke of 'a brilliant but excoriating account of incest, abuse and brutality'. Opinions such as these, which venerate the courageous and experimental elements of Lynch's work, find their roots in the steadfast beliefs of modernist criticism: the auteur may or may not be an individual engaged in social commentary, but his work still stands impressively on its own terms; pushing the aesthetic limits of institutional systems regardless of the financial penalties of doing so.

We come now though, via the biographical book, to a separate concern, one that also stems from these modernist attitudes towards art, a contradiction in fact, which if left unmanaged by the biographer, would potentially undermine our perception of the auteur's legend (where we derive it from such sources). These are the short films that do not make it onto their own DVD collections (for instance: *The Short Films of David Lynch* that features: 'Six Men Getting Sick', 'The Alphabet', 'The Grandmother', 'The Amputee', 'The Cowboy and the Frenchman', and 'Lumiere'): these are the highly lucrative commercial films produced with the specified goal of selling other people's commodities. There must be some critical aberration here because as texts these films, which are many in number, challenge any perception of Lynch as a mere 'employee'; an artisan working strictly on a wage/labour basis. We find, in fact, that Lynch's name offers commerce-defined brand identity and his promotional films are in most cases highly idiosyncratic. We will follow the argument now through our next chapter that such critical neglect is underpinned by understandings of the 'authentic' and the historically specific modernist horizons of expectation that separate art, entertainment and trade. And while the example of *Twin Peaks* has shown us that the first two domains are able to overlap (although not without some complications), we will be able to see that the intentional and open marriage of art and commerce remains a much less desirable feature in the building of artistic reputations.

CHAPTER 6

Brand Lynch

The example of *Twin Peaks* shows us that institutional corrals will impose horizonal expectations on the type of texts they tend to exhibit and that Lynch, in a sense, breached institutional rules. On the one hand, he was praised for his creative departure into the derivative prime-time soap opera before being dismissed as arrogant and self-indulgent. On the other, even within the compliant auteurist ambit of post-classical art cinema, Lynch was roundly condemned for having deviated from what was aesthetically acceptable for commercial cinema. For reasons we will come to shortly, we will reserve our analysis of the reception of *Mulholland Dr.* for the concluding chapter. But a reception study of Lynch reveals some interesting anomalies once we bring what we have learned of *Fire Walk with Me* to a conjunctural analysis of *Lost Highway* (1997), *The Straight Story* (1999) and *INLAND EMPIRE* (2006). We are able to see with *Lost Highway* the beginnings of Lynch's critical rebirth through a reversal of the standards by which he had previously been pilloried. In the example of *The Straight Story*, meanwhile, we find a film by David Lynch that wrong-footed most critics. With the latter, we are even offered a rare case study through which it is Lynch's general standing as an auteur, and his ability to spring a textual surprise, that influenced judgements of the film.

We saw in the last chapter that in blanket opposition to journalistic criticism, biographical accounts of *Fire Walk with Me* took the film up with the intent of roping Lynch's name to the proud avant-garde traditions of modern art. Indeed, although chiefly recognised as a filmmaker, in book-length biographies Lynch's legend is cemented through a proclivity to seek intertextual associations with his fine artworks (painterly, photographic and theatrical) while his numerous television commercials – including a series of four *Twin Peaks* coffee commercials for Japanese television – and other promotional films are all but passed over. By the early 1990s, and notwithstanding his humbling fall from public eminence, the term 'Lynchian' had become established in media vernacular and Lynch's name came to signify a particular commodity text; a brand no less, offering defined commercial attractions. But there remains a noticeable barrier in the building of artistic reputations that shows that the relationship between art and commerce is a difficult liaison to reconcile.

In biographical studies of Lynch, including those by Chion (1996), Hughes (2002), Rodley (1997) and Nochimson (1997), Lynch is, as we know, revered for his achievements as a filmmaker. The biographical tendency is to represent Lynch as an individual struggling against the artless commercial priorities of Hollywood, and he is, as we have long since established, celebrated as a pioneering figure of contemporary American art cinema. But in addition to his filmed enterprises, Lynch is recognised, though less well, as a fine artist (painter, sculptor, photographer), a writer/director of theatrical productions, a furniture designer, a popular music composer/producer, an animator and writer/illustrator of comic strips,[1] a television writer/producer/director (in addition to *Twin Peaks*), a web designer and a director of numerous television commercials and other promotional films.

In the task of fusing his artistic ventures, Lynch's biographers set about securing intertextual associations between Lynch's cinematic works and his creative forays into traditionally (that is in the modernist sense) refined artistic fields: namely his fine artworks (painterly, photographic and theatrical). Reference to Lynch's fine art functions with the aim of promoting Lynch within an unspecified historical evolution of modernism; with Kenneth Kaleta (1995: 3) suggesting that like 'other avant-garde filmmakers of our time' Lynch's connections with the plastic arts had provided a 'formative' and 'evolving painter's perspective' that had acted as a 'conduit for his film aesthetic'. Hughes, indeed, carried a reproduction of a 1991 article published in *Art Papers* magazine 'Organic phenomena: paintings and photographs', in which Bret Wood argued (citing Lynch's solo exhibitions in New York, Los Angeles, Tokyo, Paris and Valencia in support of his claims) a case for Lynch as an significant artist in his own right. The 'qualities that distinguish his films [...] apply to Lynch's artworks as well', he said 'and have earned him renown as a painter and photographer'. The following passage, which refers to a series of photographs that Lynch produced in the late 1980s, demonstrates this readiness to cross-associate Lynch's experimental credentials with such upright modernist practices. Wood wrote:

> In a series of 1988 photographs (*Man With Instrument, Man Thinking et al.*), the head of a toy policeman's body has been replaced with a swollen knot of chewing gum, devoid of human facial features [it is] streaked with creases like one enormous furrowed brow [...] As these works attest, the head is an anatomical portion upon which Lynch concentrates the most energy, as it is the repository of consciousness, in all its wonder and horror, and the part most sensitive to danger [...] Head trauma abounds in his filmic work (*Dune, Blue Velvet, Twin Peaks, Wild at Heart, Fire Walk with Me*) while *Eraserhead* and *Wild at Heart* feature full-blown decapitations. In non-violent situations, Lynch routinely distorts heads by lens (*Dune, Blue Velvet, Wild at Heart, Lost Highway*) and by make up (*Eraserhead, The Elephant Man*), indulging his obsession with facial disfigurement as a visual representation of interior anguish. (Hughes 2002: 257–63)

In other accounts, special mention is reserved for Lynch's theatrical production, *Industrial Symphony No. 1: The Dream of the Broken Hearted*, (performed and recorded through a multi-camera set up for video release in 1991). Chion (1996: 142) thought that *Industrial Symphony* held 'a special and very appealing place in Lynch's work' and, in 'its magical atmosphere of phantasmagorical lullaby and its visual, choreographic and musical achievements' it showed all 'the basic elements of Lynch's universe removed from its cinematic context'. Nochimson (1997: 218), meanwhile, recognised in it 'the narrative strategies of Lynch's paintings [...] its confluence of the fragments of rational realism with the flow of subconscious which is typical of the dream state'. But these biographies – which assert their authority on Lynch's films in the way they commit to looking beyond journalistic shorthand through exhaustive exegesis of the whole of his oeuvre – reinforce particular assumptions and prejudices of their own.

We are able to see that assumptions about the 'correct' constituents of art and artistic practice still circulate around the time-honoured antithetical Marxist/modernist stalling-point of art versus commodity. It is with this in mind that I want to consider Lynch's most experimental cinematic films, *Lost Highway* and *INLAND EMPIRE*, and his most unanticipated film, *The Straight Story*. But before I do this, I want to offer some analysis of Lynch's many commercials and promotional films: texts that, for the reasons I have hinted at above, are at best marginalised and at worst excluded in the formation of the Lynch canon.

Commercial Ingenuities

We start with what seems a rather rational biographical proposition: Lynch's lesser extra-cinematic incursions may function in a supporting role in the endorsement of his legend as a filmmaker. Woods (2000: 133), for instance, spoke of the television documentary series *American Chronicles*[2] as a show that 'may well be ripe for revival every now and then, to compare its gentle, sincere views of everyday quirkiness against the sensational prurience of vintage Mondo'. But Lynch's commercial and promotional films tend only to be annotated, if they are annotated at all, in filmographies ('Advertising Spots' in Chion's example).

We can, in fact, divide Lynch's promotional work into two overlapping categories. In the first category it is Lynch's kudos as an artist that will act as an endorsement for a given product. In the second category the product comes to the fore and it is Lynch's aesthetic style that helps to distinguish that product within the marketplace. And while Lynch is, of course, hired on the strength of his cinematic artistry, we should not forget, either, that he has earned himself a reputation as an accomplished technician able to bring high standards of professionalism to his work.

Before we come to his apparent advertisements, we find that Lynch has also directed a small number of music videos that, although their purpose might be cleverly concealed, are conceived, all the same, to sell related music products. Indeed, promotional videos can attract a certain artistic cachet for themselves and can be sold on as downloads or collections and are even the subject of their own annual awards ceremonies (the MTV Music Awards, for instance). However, while promotional films might be in themselves of aesthetic interest, the musicians keep one hand firmly on the artistic baton and should not be usurped by the video director. Directors and musicians may also enhance their good taste and standing through these collaborations.

In fact, it has become quite commonplace for auteurs to direct music videos and their creative involvement, like Lynch's 30-second promotional trailer for Michael Jackson's 'Black or White' (1991) film, can function through publicity as a creative endorsement in its own right.

Jackson, as is well known, made the world's best selling music album, *Thriller*, in 1983. The title track became a landmark 14-minute mini film (directed, like 'Black or White', by John Landis), which culminated in the morphing of Jackson from human to (dancing) werewolf. Landis had honed this spectacular technical feat on his 1981 movie, *An American Werewolf in London*. Jackson's following album, *Bad* (1986), repeated the auteurist formula, this time employing Martin Scorsese to direct the promo for the title song (as a choreographed gangland standoff on a New York subway). Jackson followed in 1991 with *Dangerous*, a year or so before Lynch's critical stock was to reach its nadir. It is even-handed to presume, though, that the disquieting properties of Lynch's surrealistic worldview may have jarred with the global image Sony wanted to promote for its flagship artist (Jackson).

Nonetheless, writing for *The Independent*, John Gallivan (1991) reported that since the 'Thriller' video still loomed 'over the history of rock', the promotion for 'Black or White' had to be 'something extra'. For a reputed fee of $1.5m, Gallivan continued, 'David Lynch obliged and came up' with what he called a 'promo with a promo of its own: a trailer' that took shape in a '30 seconds lead into the $6m, 11-minute ['Black or White'] spectacular'. The fact that Lynch did not direct 'Black or White' (the first promo for *Dangerous*) did not matter, given that Lynch's peripheral involvement in the project generated publicity that unreservedly supported the theory that Jackson remained at the cutting edge as an artist.

In a similar fashion to the endorsement of Jackson, Lynch's name worked as a product approval for two print advertisements that merit our attention. In both examples – the first produced towards the end of the 1990s, the second in 2000 (by which time, as we shall see shortly, Lynch had undergone something of a critical rebirth) – we can observe how explicit and implicit understandings of what an artist represents are exploited to commercial ends. The first (for the Technics 'Home Cinema Range') trades on Lynch's name and image explicitly. Through a photomontage featuring Lynch and signifiers associated with the darker elements of his films, we are advised that 'when David Lynch invites you to lend him your ears ask for a receipt' and that the 'Technics AX7 AV receiver reveals the full range of this sorcerer of cineaste's dark arts'. The second example, for American Express credit cards, would appear a little more provocative in that it rebelliously collides the worlds of art and commodities – commodities, no less, that we can charge to a credit card. In this example, we are neither told nor reminded that this is David Lynch; we rely only on his image and text that reads: 'Visionary Since 81' and 'Are You a Card member?'. Small print does, however, reassure us that American Express is donating funds to the American Film Institute, which would seem to seek to imply that Lynch's personal motivations for agreeing to the advertisement were artistically and not monetarily motivated. Nevertheless, and while we may or may not recognise Lynch (the perceptive consumer would be in on the scheme, or, if they did not recognise Lynch, then they may feel confronted by the feeling of cultural inferiority since a 'visionary' who doesn't need naming must surely be of great magnitude), his image – a little wizened and non-conformist in his unruly mane and raised and buttoned collar – connotes the shared artistic and capitalist values of individualism and freedom (an image at odds, incidentally, with the conservative descriptions often commented upon in the earlier stages of his career).

We find, though, that despite these common values, it is precisely in the prejudicial tension between commodities and art that the neglect of Lynch's commercial films can be traced. The auteurist critic may tend to defend the omission of Lynch's promotional films from his canon on the unwritten understanding that his television commercials are merely generic, artisanal endeavours, conducted on a wage/labour basis. But bearing in mind that it is always advertising's role to distinguish its product in one way or another, we find that a number of Lynch's commercials are in fact highly idiosyncratic and have even been referred to by Lynch as 'little bitty films' (Rodley 1997: 211).

In a book that totals some 270 pages, *Lynch on Lynch* gives over only two pages to his commercials. Rodley engages Lynch over his work on several fragrance commercials.[3] Lynch reveals that he is 'not against them [commercials in general]' and that he 'always learns something by doing them'. Fragrance commercials (for the likes of Calvin Klein, Giorgio Armani, Yves Saint Laurent, Jill Sanders and Gucci) are one thing, but – and if we are prepared to accept Rodley's line of questioning as an indicator for a wider critical prejudice – it would appear within acceptable limits for the auteur to earn money as an employee working on commercials, but on the proviso

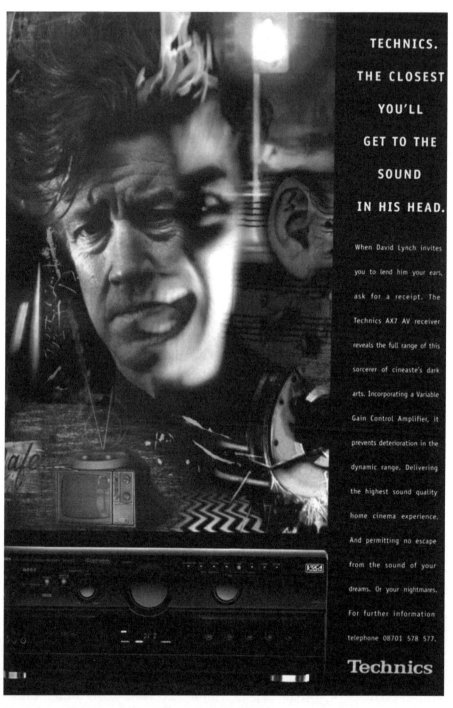

Technics and American Express: auteur as product endorsement.

VISIONARY SINCE

81

ARE YOU A CARDMEMBER?

American Express is pleased to donate a $25,000 scholarship in David's name to the American Film Institute to help young filmmakers.

that these be separated out from the true artworks.[4] On this note, Rodley expressed particular concern over a series of four commercials Lynch produced for the Japanese tinned coffee company, Georgia Coffee, in 1991.

Tapping directly into *Twin Peaks*, and Agent Cooper's 'damn fine coffee' catchphrase, these commercials featured a number of the original cast members who combined in the story of a Japanese man's search for his missing wife (with, of course, the help of Special Agent Cooper).[5] So while we might recall that Rodley (and all Lynch's biographers for that matter) were undisturbed by Lynch's decision to expand *Twin Peaks* into a feature film, Rodley wanted to know from Lynch if it was 'at all a concern to take something like *Peaks* and make an ad' since, Rodley surmised, this 'might undermine some of the seriousness or the magic of the series?'. Lynch, in fact, fell into line with Rodley's mood of disquiet: 'I'm really against it in principle, but they were so much fun to do, and they were only running in Japan and so it just felt OK.' 'So you wouldn't have done them for the American market?', Rodley continued, to which Lynch replied 'No, I don't think so.'[6] The relevance of national markets is not immediately forthcoming but what is apparent is that Lynch felt that he could abandon his serious

Agent Cooper, Georgia Coffee commercial.

artistic responsibilities overseas without damaging his reputation at home. This exchange might even invite further speculations, but, in any event, it offers us an indicator of the unspoken accord that prefers that poetics and trade be kept as separate affairs in the practices of legend making.

It would appear that the salient reason for such a mind-set is part of a standard that stems from a modernist/Marxist criticism that stigmatises commodities and their fetishisation (through commercials in our examples). This is a point I will come back to, but not before I address the wider critical neglect of these texts as legitimate auteurist works. Discussions and articles on these commercials are not so uncommon in the press. Indeed, picking up on the 'Clear Blue Easy' pregnancy test advertisement, in which a young woman is seen anxiously waiting for her results as a clock-face ticks between 'Yes' and 'No' (text that replaces the clock-face's numerical characters), *Entertainment Weekly* carried an article that recognised a thematic Lynchian preoccupation and speculated thus that Lynch was 'attracted to the advertisement because it involves the psychological torture of a beautiful young woman' (Jacobs 1997). But even other, European commercials which more intentionally exploit proverbial Lynchian themes and motifs do not merit recognition as auteurist texts.

Writing about 'The Wall', produced by the advertising agency Leagus and Delaney on behalf of the German sportswear company Adidas in 1993, for instance, Nicholas Ind (1993) reported for *The Guardian* that Lynch had been hired by Adidas with the aim of getting 'the young to re-appraise the brand – without losing the hard-core sports enthusiast'. 'The problem' facing Adidas, Ind reasoned 'was not one of product – it is well respected by top athletes – but of image'. While Adidas's major competitors (namely Nike and Reebok) 'had spent millions on advertising and star endorsements', 'The Wall', 'an off-beat film which shows the hell and heaven a long distance runner experiences in going through the pain barrier (represented by a wall)', was Adidas's first British television commercial in nine years.

Ind suggested that Lynch's advert, at a fee 'close to $1million', was remarkable not for the size of the fee but because 'cult filmmakers don't make TV advertisements [since] they tend to be too iconoclastic and anti-consumerist'. Ind remarked, in fact, that it would be difficult 'to imagine a [Jean-Luc] Godard car commercial'. (While we may endorse Ind's general sentiment, a Swiss advertising campaign featuring commercials by Lynch, Godard, Enki Bilal, Emir Kusturica and Giuseppe Tornatore for

Parisienne cigarettes did in fact run in Swiss cinemas from 1998. Indeed, Lynch's commercial is even *signed*: 'by David Lynch'.[7]) Still, Lynch's own brand identity, which would readily eschew 'product story' in favour of 'surreal images of the athlete's mind and body', suited Adidas' needs since the company was not concerned with 'communicating product values' but sought, rather, to 'entertain its market'. Ind concluded, in fact, that 'market research in France, Germany, Spain and the UK suggests that the teenage market like[d] and [understood] the work, although the exact meaning of "Earn Them" [a military reference to the Adidas 'three stripe' logo] sometimes escape[d] them'.

The fallacious assumption that exists within auteurist discourse that true artists should be somehow above commercial interests is widely manifest. But in an annotation, Hughes describes how Sony's creative director Trevor Beattie insisted that 'Lynch was the only choice' for the titled European cinema commercial 'The Third Place' (2000), an advertisement for Sony's Playstation 2 (PS2) games console that is dense with Lynchian adornments. Hughes in fact describes a 60-second cinema commercial 'in which a young man enters "the third place" where he meets a doppelganger of himself, a bandaged man – and a talking duck!' (2002: 268). Lynch had also contributed a series of shorter films for the PS2 television campaign including: 'Different place different rules', a film in which a speeding car crashes into a stationary deer, destroying the car while the deer walks off unscathed and unperturbed, and 'Visit your third place', a film of a sleeping dog whose legs twitch furiously as he or she dreams (of chasing rabbits perhaps).[8] The value of the Lynch brand to industry was encapsulated in a press release for carmaker Nissan's 2002 European Micra commercial.

Nissan stated that 'so original and distinctive is its new Micra' that the company had 'invented a new language to describe it. And our teacher [of that language] will be David Lynch'. Nissan described the Micra as 'no ordinary car', and as such 'no ordinary words can communicate it'. Between them, Nissan and Lynch had developed a 'fusion of existing words to create a whole new vocabulary, such as modern yet retro – to make modtro'. In the same release, Lynch spoke of the influence of surrealist artist René Magritte 'who put lips in the sky' (the film features a pair of giant floating blue lips that speak the word 'modtro') and the 'feel of those big beautiful lips speaking in a supermodern and very graphic city [Paris]'. Concluding, Nissan's Creative Director, Chris Garbutt, remarked that in fact Lynch had filmed the car 'in a way reminiscent of the way he shot women in *Twin Peaks* and *Mulholland Drive*: with mystery, sensuality and with a sense of the bizarre'.[9]

In her well-known essay 'But I know what I like...the function of art in advertising', Judith Williamson (1987: 69–73) suggested that a given advertisement's reference to art (although presumably this might also occur through direct citation as with the example Magritte's lips) as 'an art structure' will communicate to the public 'the genuinely "cultured" status of the ads, and, therefore, of the product'. But for Williamson this union was not a happy one since she viewed commercial appropriations of high art as being shot through with an inverted 'social snobbery'. If we follow this attitude through Miles Orvell, we may recognise that the ill feeling towards the commercial appropriation of art is itself a direct consequence of trade interests. 'The concept of authenticity', Orvell (1989: xv–xvii) argued 'begins in any society when the possibility of fraud arises, and that fraud is at least possible whenever transactions – whether social, political, commercial, or aesthetic routinely occur'. Orvell finds in the late nineteenth/early twentieth

Nissan Micra commercial.

century, moreover, an epochal (or horizonal paradigm) shift in intuitive assessments of value since 'the culture of authenticity that developed at the end of the [nineteenth] century' and which 'established the aesthetic vocabulary that we have called modernist' and reflected 'an effort to get beyond mere imitation, beyond the manufacturing of illusions, to the creation of more "authentic" works that were themselves the real thing'.

Whatever the aesthetic merits of the text, commercial advertising becomes, under any kind of critical scrutiny, a palpable demonstration of the 'manufacturing of illusions'. It goes against the grain to think of these films as auteurist because the advertising film's function (and therefore its status) remains unchanging and unambiguous. Advertising, in other words, *can only ever be an illusion* and so lacks the potential for fraud to arise. The same rules do not apply to cinema, where the auteurist text must carry a degree of ambiguity for it to fulfil the need to be authenticated through a signature to begin with. Indeed, this is only possible because the status of cinema moves between illusionist and realist modes of production. Tom Gunning (1986) drew the distinction between a narrative cinema, whereby the audience is drawn into the illusion of a fictitious filmed world, and a 'cinema of attractions', whereby the absorption process is confronted and the audience is challenged to wonder about some sort of extra-textual reality. It has become the modern auteurist's task to plot a critical route between the two paths.

Before we move on to discuss the importance of the Lynch brand to his cinematic projects, we should, given that Lynch described it as falling somewhere 'between a regular film and a commercial', pause to consider *Lady Blue Shanghai*, a short film that launched on the Christian Dior website in May 2010. This 17-minute advertising event even carried its own double-page promotional spread which appeared in quality fashion magazines (including *Vogue* in its June 2010 issue). The film was marketed in the manner of an authored cinematic film: 'Dior presents Marion Cotillard in *Lady Blue Shanghai*, a film directed by David Lynch [and] inspired by John Galliano'. Reporting in the *Financial Times* on the eve of the film's launch, Nicola Copping (2010) explained how Dior had in fact offered Lynch free creative reign so long as the film showed 'the [Dior] handbag, the Pearl Tower [in Shanghai] and some old Shanghai'. For Lynch, it was an offer that allowed him to work in 'a new advertising genre devoid of heavy-handed branding' that was appealing. For Galliano, it was Lynch who brought 'the style, the mystery, the suspense' to the Dior product.

Lady Blue Shanghai, described in the article as 'oblique, enigmatic, weird but wonderful [and] crammed with Lynchian leitmotifs', features Marion Cotillard:

> tiptoeing along a deserted corridor in a deserted Shanghai hotel. Music is blaring from her room. She opens the door, terror etched across her face, to find a bag (yes, it's the Lady Dior!) – blue, square, on a pedestal, a light beaming behind it. Two security guards arrive to investigate and [...] she slips into a dream-like state. The bag has triggered the memory of febrile kisses exchanged between her and a Chinese paramour in front of Shanghai's Pearl Tower, and of his hurried escape, handing her a blue rose as he flees. She awakens, a tear trickling down her powdered cheek. She inches towards the bag, opens the clasp, looks inside and finds the blue rose.[10]

We cannot predict how *Lady Blue Shanghai* might be treated in future biographical accounts of Lynch. But given its duration (should that be a factor in determining auteurist value) and the fact that the 'commercial aspect of the film has been diluted (the word Dior is notably absent)' in an effort to 'enhance the brand's artistic credibility', then the traditional biographer will be presented with a very contemporary auteurist impediment. If *Lady Blue Shanghai* is to be considered for bona-fide auteur status, then the auteurist will need to consider carefully its modes of exhibition, given that in order to watch the film, the viewer is first directed to a Christian Dior website, a practice of which Copping (2010) remarked: 'what better way to expose a brand's sensitive, intellectual, artsy side? Goodbye sell! sell! sell!, hello linger! savour! appreciate the art! (and then buy the perfume)' (sic).

Our discussion has reached a point historically where Lynch had become a dependable brand name within the industry and amongst the public. And having established the value of Lynch's sign to advertising (notwithstanding the fact that his name would be overshadowed by the name of the product) we can show that his sign is of the utmost commercial importance in the cinematic sphere too. Indeed, without Lynch's name to herald its arrival, it is hard to imagine how a film such as *INLAND EMPIRE* – a film described in *Time Out* as taking 'the tag "Lynchian" to new levels' (Calhoun 2007) – would be marketed generically, if, indeed, production costs could have been raised for a film of this type in the first place. Auteurism *is* about selling, but an author's name is these days such a regular feature in marketing and publicity that it might be that the author function can only become meaningful historically once such promotional ephemera is measured against the properties of the text(s) it represents. All the same, cinema is an institution that accommodates art and entertainments, so issues of authenticity must always address themselves to the limits of genre over institutional restraints even if, as in the case of Lynch, the poetic boundaries of that institution will be put to the test.

An Auteurist Renaissance

In making his case for the inclusion of Michael Curtiz in the pantheon of classical auteurs, Peter Wollen took his discussion back to the quarrel between Bazin and the younger critics at *Cahiers du Cinéma*. As Wollen notes (2003: 65–74), Bazin saw the auteur as 'a quintessential genre artist, accepting conventions and stereotypes while pursuing his or her personal predilections within the permissible constraints'. From this Wollen surmised that 'if the genre constraints were overlooked or brushed aside, the result would be [for Bazin] a flawed film, whereas for the younger *Cahiers* critics it would be an auteurist masterpiece'. Wollen believed that Curtiz was scorned (if that isn't too harsh a term) as a 'hack' by the *Cahiers* writers because of his generic adaptability. And Hawks and Hitchcock, Wollen reminds us, had their reputations fastened, respectively, if not exclusively, as directors of westerns and suspense thrillers. 'The case for Curtiz as an auteur', Wollen continues, stands upon 'his incredible ability to find the right style for the right picture' while he was still able to express a 'thematic consistency across several genres [...] in his consistent preference for stressing the struggle of the rebel or the downtrodden against the entrenched and the powerful'. I am deliberately conflating different industrial contexts here since it is necessary to establish dictated working freedoms under different systems. Curtiz is associated with the vertically integrated studio system (and with Warner Bros. Studios more often than not) while Lynch is representative of lateral post-classical systems and its independent production arms.

In casting Curtiz in the classical auteurist model (the individual who struggles against the system), Wollen correlates Curtiz's authorship with issues of control. He pursues the line, through Jack Stillinger, that 'many recognized auteurs were writer-directors or writer-producers or in a position to get their own way, as Curtiz was, because of their prestige, obstinacy, negotiating skills, or capacity for intimidation'. Classical auteurs succeeded, Wollen continued (2003: 70) 'because of their pivotal position in the production process' and 'because they fight, as Curtiz did, to exercise control over script changes, casting decisions, set design, editing, and even camera position and shots'.

Lynch occupies a position within an aesthetically dispersed post-classical system in which he is able to work under much greater freedoms than Curtiz and his contemporaries. We might remember, for instance, that in addition to his role as a director – and with the privilege over final cut most of the time – Lynch is a writer or co-writer and sometimes producer, sometimes actor and sometimes even score composer for his films. So while there are other important industrial and creative collaborations in the raw authorship of Lynch's films (Freddie Francis, Kyle MacLachlan, Laura Dern, Angelo Badalamenti, Mary Sweeny, Barry Gifford and StudioCanal spring most readily to mind), if the case is to be made for a salient agent in the interpretation of films, then Lynch, like a dedicated number of other post-classical auteurs, would cut a more persuasive figure than Curtiz and other auteurs working within the classical system.

I will return to this issue. However, even if we say for the time being that we do accept Lynch as the ruling agency in the interpretation of his films, other conflicts still exist. To return once more to the genre/auteur struggle that occupies Wollen's study of Curtiz: in this respect, we still need to keep in mind the distinction between the public figure of the post-classical auteur (e.g. Lynch) and the largely concealed existence of his/her classical antecedents (e.g. Curtiz). The auteur is, in other words, no longer the private property of a filmic academy but a dialogic sign – similar to the examples of Lynch's commercial films since its job is to distinguish a product – to be exchanged in the transaction between producers and consumers. But as I will demonstrate in my analysis of *Mulholland Dr.* in the following chapter, the author will typically function as one part of a 'promotional cluster' of humanist and generic textual pledges that vie for the audience's affections. In laying the foundations for that discussion, I want to turn the remainder of this chapter over to the reception of Lynch's interim cinematic works, *Lost Highway* (1997), *The Straight Story* (1999) and *INLAND EMPIRE*, his most recent picture.

It is adequate for my argument at this stage to say that these three features are more auteurist than *Mulholland Dr.* The production details for

Mulholland Dr. are quite unusual so bring to light auteurist complications that I will explore over the reach of that chapter. We could in fact make similar categorical problems for the auteurist readings of *Lost Highway*, *The Straight Story* and *INLAND EMPIRE*. But we will suspend this line of analysis for the time being and focus our thoughts on establishing Lynch and the auteur as signifying agents in their own right. These three films are well placed to separate out the sub-generic and generic categories 'Lynchian' and 'auteurist' since *Lost Highway* and *INLAND EMPIRE* are generally regarded as two of Lynch's most oblique, and therefore most 'Lynchian', works. For auteurist critics, *The Straight Story* remains his most unanticipated film. Indeed, although it is a path we will not follow, should we have been inclined to do so we might have expected to come across fresh implications for the author and his role in textual pleasure (according to Barthes's reading model) since *The Straight Story* has the potential to bring about a crisis through an authorial reading paradigm.

We saw in the journalistic reception of *Fire Walk with Me* that the hostility directed towards the film was based partly on what was perceived as Lynch's brazen indifference to principles of comprehensible narrative, and because of this fact, *Fire Walk with Me* ignored the rules for rewarding cinema. Yet with the release of *Lost Highway*, a film co-written with Barry Gifford that seemed to hang on a loose generic description of a contemporary LA noir, those same formal characteristics – more pronounced, even, in a film regarded at that time as Lynch's most defiant narrative to date – were being reappraised. That is not to say that the film was not received with an air of resigned confusion. The problem facing most critics was that *Lost Highway* was, as *Variety* observed, just 'too deliberately obscure' (McCarthy 1997). Judgements on the text, if they were formed at all, were based, like those on *Fire Walk with Me*, on the formal appropriateness of *Lost Highway* as a cinematic artwork and, as the upshot of this, Lynch's threatened credentials as an auteur.

Firstly, then, critics like Geoff Andrew (1997) asked where the film sat as entertainment given 'its suddenly and inexplicably metamorphosed protagonist, its various doubles, and a narrative structure that may be described as a circle, a spiral or even a figure of eight'. Andrew concluded that audiences were faced with two choices: 'either dismiss the film as pretentious rubbish or to try and make sense of it on a metaphorical level'. Reporting on the film's reception at its premiere in France, Kate Muir (1997) echoed the above sentiments in suggesting that while some critics had 'hailed Lynch as "one of greatest image makers of the epoch" [others] felt they had lost two-and-a-half hours of their lives they would never regain'. Geoff Brown (1998), meanwhile, thought that *Lost Highway*'s 'universe [was] so extreme, so brazen in refusing rational explanations, that audiences [could] either hitch [...] to Lynch's wagon and bask in [its] perverse delights' or 'stand outside alienated from a film that talks a private language'. *Lost Highway* did, however, mark a turning point at which Lynch's critical reputation began to pick up.

Remembering that five years earlier Lynch had been brought to task for being over arty and too self-indulgent, critics now detected a single-mindedness that provided a shot in the arm for his artistic veracity. Lynch, it seemed, had demonstrated integrity in sticking to his aesthetic principles. Donald Lyons (1997) was one who spoke of *Lost Highway* as a 'painter's movie' in which 'the whole alluring, baffling film [was] a sensuous marvel [by an] eccentric, pioneering sensibility conquering new and savage territory for his art'. For Ryan Gilby (1997), the film was one of his 'Moments that made the year' and he described 'Lynch's breathtaking comeback [as] the kind of daring picture that a director only usually has the guts to make at the start of his career or during exile'. Dennis Lim (1997) even sought to persuade his readers that Lynch was 'one of cinema's great expressionists: an expert in finding the exact visual and aural textures for sinister, barely communicable moods and sensations'.

Typically for films bearing his name, we find in the above examples that the pre-eminence of Lynch's agency was the characteristic reading aspect of *Lost Highway*. But the wider demands placed on the auteur can be more clearly illustrated if we consider *Lost Highway* in a conjunctural analysis with his subsequent release, *The Straight Story*. This activity will underline the point I have already made, that the post-classical auteur and Lynch might be thought of in terms of overlapping horizonal paradigms: that is generic (auteurist) and sub-generic (Lynchian). What we find in this comparison is that so contrary were the structural properties of the two films that these categories demanded to be read almost as discrete reading paradigms. *The Straight Story*, in other words, was so 'straight' that it defeated horizons of expectation for a David Lynch film.

We have established that *Lost Highway* was read as an archetypal Lynchian text since, as Mike Higgins's (1998) apt witticism reminded us 'demanding narrative clarity from a David Lynch film [was] like bemoaning the lack of good car chase at the end of *The Seventh Seal*'. And when word reached the media that Lynch's next feature would be an adaptation of the true story (widely reported in the US media) of a 73-year-old man, Alvin Straight (played in the film by Richard Farnsworth), who, seeking reconciliation with an estranged brother, journeyed across Middle America on a lawnmower, horizonal expectations were duly established. Reporting on the project a year prior to its release for instance, Clive King (1998) predicted that 'Alvin Straight's six-week, five miles-per-hour mission of mercy sounds like something from a David Lynch movie – and indeed it soon will be'. Yet no one reckoned on Lynch's treatment of his material. On this occasion it was the very absence of a Lynchian worldview that merited critical attention.

Staiger (2003: 35) noted that 'the authorship – as-personality approach' develops 'the standard assumption [...] that the *body* of the director ensures a unified perspective on the world, and repetition is where the critic finds the director's perspective'. But with *The Straight Story*, Lynch had pulled off something of a horizonal deception. Such was the perceived dearth of Lynchian worldview in *The Straight Story* that critics were compelled to discuss Lynch almost exclusively in terms of a generalised auteurist standing. That is not to say that Lynch's authorship was corrupted; quite the reverse in fact. With *Lost Highway* we saw that Lynch was lauded for sticking to his artistic principles in the face of undisputed critical defamation. This, though, was a reversal of that standard; the contrary criterion that heaps scorn on the artist who tries to repeat, or 'cash in' on previous glories. So with *The Straight Story* it was not so much the repetition of the director's unified perspective as the variation of that perspective that garnered critical praise.

While it is true to say that the release of *The Straight Story* prompted a mild tone of scepticism in some quarters – the *LA Times* (Turan 1999), for instance, thought 'the equivalent of David Lynch doing "Little House on the Prairie" (sic)' was a rather 'suspect enterprise' – the wider feeling was that *The Straight Story* was an auteurist work of rare individualism. Jonathan Romney even thought that the film 'may be one of the riskiest ventures ever undertaken by a major director' since it threatened to 'strike a cord with audiences who would normally be repelled by Lynch's febrile visions, while perplexing long-term fans' at the same time (Romney 1999). As an illustration of this point, Christopher Heyn (1999), writing for the online journal *Christian Spotlight on the Movies*, awarded *The Straight Story* a 5/5 score and its highest moral rating, and, in praising 'the compassion that Lynch [had shown] for his characters', prompted 'the "Christian community" [to] get out and support motion pictures of this quality'.

In its wider reception the likes of Anthony Quinn (1999) were reporting that 'that it's a film by David Lynch is enough to make you choke on your doughnut': 'no severed ears', he asked 'no helium-gobbling psychopaths, no dancing dwarves? Can this really be David Lynch'?. Writing for *The Independent*, Rodley (1999) thought it 'truly shocking' that *The Straight Story* 'did not disturb, offend or mystify [...] surely', he reasoned 'there was just a little filicide? Some incest maybe?'. Gilbert Adair (1999) seemed to sum up the general feeling towards Lynch and his movie, meanwhile, when he spoke of *The Straight Story* as a 'perplexing paradox'; an 'extremely curious cinematic object, of initial interest, like Dr Johnson's performing dog, because of its very existence', and was thus left to reflect on an auteur who 'had pulled off a seldom-achieved ideal' in making a movie that was 'both completely personal and completely different from any other in his filmography'. But what might we draw from the comparison between these films? And how does it help us to begin to address the author in the writing of a multifaceted film history?

We witnessed, through Wollen's assessment of Curtiz, a determined attempt to detach the author from the generic curb of the system. Wollen applauded the malleability of Curtiz's worldview that was, in his assessment, forcibly rewritten across a range of generic staples. This matter of a perceived worldview is one that takes us back to the earliest debates on the merits of auteurism. To sanction the auteur through stylistic traits was one thing, given the counter argument proposed by Ian Cameron (1981: 52) that 'Hollywood films are not so much custom-built as manufactured', and that a film's 'final quality [...] is no more the fault of the director than as of such parties as [...] the set designer, the camera man and the hairdresser', but to proffer critical speculation upon thematic consistencies drifted, for Cameron, too far away from the observational responsibilities of the critic.

Cameron's concerns resounded in the pages of the British journal *Movie*, first published in 1962. Through the editorships of Cameron, Mark Shivas, Paul Mayersberg and Victor Perkins, *Movie*'s criticism restricted a film's analysis to formal specifications. Caughie (1981: 49–50), indeed, saw *Movie*'s dependency on 'an appeal to an underlined common sense' as its Achilles' heel, since it gave rise to the potential for a lack of any discernable critical development, 'a lack of development, that is to say, relative to the shifting conjuncture of film and cultural criticism'. All the same, in the second edition of *Movie*, Cameron (1981: 52) expressed what he saw as a hindrance in *la politique*'s preference for thematic authorial intertexts:

> On the whole we accept the cinema of directors, although without going to the farthest-out extremes of *la politique des auteurs* which makes it difficult to think of a bad director making a good film and almost impossible to think of a good director making a bad one. One's aesthetic must be sufficiently flexible to cope with the fact that Joseph Pevney, having made dozens of stinkers, can suddenly come up with an admirable western in *The Plunderers*, or that Minnelli, after years of doing wonders often with unpromising material, could produce anything as flat footed as *The Bells are Ringing*.

In the same piece Cameron (1981: 55), like Wollen some 40 years on, spoke highly of *Casablanca* ('something really remarkable'). Yet unlike Wollen (2003: 75–76), who believed *Casablanca* showed Curtiz to be a director 'who rose to the occasion' – a director 'who could wring unexpected meanings from a script' while at the same time showing a 'confident sense of style, in composition, in performance and in editing' – Cameron (1981: 55) was insistent that *Casablanca*'s merits were to be located in the efforts of 'an efficient director' working with 'magnificent collaborators'. In the first place, this difference of opinion illustrates the uneven nature of aesthetic readings that will vary both historically and from critic to critic. But it also points to historical auteurist differences, since ideas of control, which are contested under the classical system, and agency, which are assumed under the post-classical system, make quite different critical demands on the auteur.

If we look back one last time at the differences of opinion over the merits of *Fire Walk with Me*, we see that the issue of control (or agency) is not what is at stake. Journalistic assessments saw the film as fraudulent, not because it was not Lynchian, but because the perception was that Lynch was motivated by profit, and thus sought to exploit his audience through formulaic auteurist repetitions. Biographical assessments, which are auteurist in any event, presented the film as the 'real thing' since Lynch was seen to do quite the reverse in challenging that audience. In either case, *Fire Walk with Me* must declare its agency since it was a text that had opened up a space for its cinematic value to be contested.

While it is usually incumbent upon film criticism to navigate the balance between genre and humanist preferences (and there is no reason why it should not), with *INLAND EMPIRE* there appeared very little other option than to read the film as a Lynchian affair. While this statement is not absolutely conclusive, the mood certainly prevails that the film can *only* appeal to Lynch aficionados, since there are no other obvious points of intertextual stability.

In 2006 Lynch published *Catching the Big Fish: Meditation, Consciousness, and Creativity*. In it, Lynch explains how transcendental meditation had offered him 'a way to dive deeper in search of the big fish', which he offers as an analogy for his search for creative ideas. For Lynch, then, this search is essentially an inward looking process, a narcissistic tendency that, according to Freud, is a common characteristic shared by artists (Freud 1950). Lynch (2006: 1–2) describes, moreover, how his 'thirty-three year practice of the Transcendental Meditation program has been central to [his] work in painting and to all areas of [his] life' (although, it seems, only more recently has he started to publicise the fact widely).

In the case of *INLAND EMPIRE* 'the big fish' showed itself initially in the form of a 14-page monologue Lynch had written for Laura Dern and which he filmed (digitally) in a single, 70-minute take. Lynch proceeds to describe how a 'secret' to a story emerged from Dern's 'phenomenal' performance and from his belief that seemingly unrelated scenes can be linked through a 'unified field': 'the ocean is the unity and these things float on it', he wrote. Indeed, Lynch summarised the production process for *INLAND EMPIRE* thus:

> We shot it entirely on digital video so the level of flexibility and control was amazing. Also, I didn't have a script. I wrote the thing scene by scene, without much of a clue where it would end. It was a risk, but I had this feeling that because all things are unified, this idea over here would somehow relate to that idea over there. And I was working with a very great company, StudioCanal in France, who believed in me – enough to let me find my way.
> (Lynch 2006: 141–45)

In the same book, Lynch remarked that he thought it 'totally absurd' that filmmakers should have to compromise their vision and that the filmmaker 'should decide every single element, every single word, every single sound, every single thing going down that highway through time. Otherwise it [the film] won't hold together' (Lynch 2006: 60). But while we might wish

INLAND EMPIRE promotional poster.

to rejoice in the liberating sense of artistic expression Lynch was able to bring to the screen, it seems quite reasonable to speculate that Lynch was only allowed to 'find his way' by StudioCanal because of the relatively low production costs of shooting digitally, and because the film could be pre-sold (especially in Europe) on Lynch's auteurist eminence, which was no longer a matter of any serious dispute anyway following the commercial and critical triumphs of *Mulholland Dr.* (a film also financed by the French company). It comes as no surprise therefore, that Lynch declared 'I love the French. They're the biggest film buffs and protectors of cinema in the world' (Lynch 2006: 59).

Given the above, it seems remarkable that *Variety* was able to report from the 2006 Venice Film Festival on 'frisky international sales' for a film it described as so 'murky' and 'unattractive' that 'even arthouses may find it difficult to keep aud[iences] in seats' (Weissberg 2006). This is surely testament to the commercial attractions of the author, especially when we consider that *The Hollywood Reporter* was commenting on a film that 'lasts three hours and seems to last longer' and, notwithstanding 'occasional startling images', was an 'interminable bore [...] filled with dreary sequences in poor lighting [and] incongruous scenes featuring characters who are never explained'. It was unsurprising, then, that the trade paper predicted a box office appeal 'limited to Lynch devotees and the contentedly bewildered' (Bennet 2006).

In light of *INLAND EMPIRE*'s design, and its lack of fixed generic reference points, there seemed no rational alternative but to read the film as a Lynchian picture. The IMDb pointed to the difficulty of the task at hand in marrying the following 'plot keywords' for the film:

> Actress, Hollywood, cigarette smoking, dress, film within a film, mysticism, blood splatter, end of the world, circus, tear on cheek, blood, applause, stabbed in the chest, cult favorite, debt, death, dance number, breaking the fourth wall, silk, barbecue, class difference, mysterious villain, experimental film, prostitution, murder, female nudity, stream of consciousness, gore, clown, rabbit suit, parallel story, infidelity, curse, avant-garde, gun, insanity, conflated realities, stabbed in the stomach, surrealism, alternative reality, film title spoken by character. (Inland Empire keywords)

INLAND EMPIRE delivers us to a point at which generic and auteurist relations become intractable. Given such a state of affairs, we may reasonably enough come back to the longstanding criticism of auteurism that it is socially divisive and there would be a strong case to be made for that argument if we were to isolate *INLAND EMPIRE* as a text which will only appeal to Lynch devotees. But that a film of this kind could secure a commercial release at all tells us something about our ongoing fascination with the figure of the auteur and, indeed, the current state of cinema as institution since this film, not unlike *Fire Walk with Me* and *Lost Highway*, put to the test some kind of notional cut-off point for what passes as cinematic art. Auteurist films do not usually do this, however. We stand to gain a more measured view therefore, of the day-to-day function of the contemporary auteur, if we turn our attention finally to Lynch's previous picture, *Mulholland Dr.*, a film marketed by StudioCanal as 'A contemporary film noir, directed by David Lynch'.

CHAPTER 7

Receiving *Mulholland Dr.*: 'A Contemporary Film Noir Directed by David Lynch'[1]

In her book *Perverse Spectators*, published at the start of the new millennium, Staiger (2000: 24) suggested that film studies was compelled to ask 'two major questions about the history and nature of cinema'. These were: 'what are the experiences of cinema viewing for the audiences?' and 'what are the meanings of those experiences?'. In keeping with the tone of Staiger's declarations, we have tried in his book to present a more comprehensive picture of the audience's experiences of the aesthetic text. Indeed, our aim in undertaking what we have ventured to call a 'textual historicity' has been to contribute something close to what Staiger called, 'a historical affective and cognitive epistemology and aesthetics of cinema'. In backing these principles – and in doing so without neglecting the text – we have attempted to bypass some of the restrictions that have oppressed auteurism in one way or other over its history. We turn now, then, to *Mulholland Dr.*, an authored film that, if we approach by accounting for the interdependencies of modes of production, exhibition, promotion and criticism, gives us a good chance of forming an understanding of how the modern audience may assemble the contemporary aesthetic text.

Following the break up of cine-structuralism in the early 1970s, quite how one could reconnect objectively with authored texts other than historically had set theorists tough hermeneutic challenges. In my discussion of *Blue Velvet* in Chapter 4, I showed that since the 1990s some esteemed scholars have made committed cases for causality for certain texts. We may recall that Kobena Mercer, Andy Medhurst and Staiger (a historian and possibly the leading figure in filmic reception studies) all backed the principle of 'agency in the cultural struggle' (Mercer 1991: 181). In the same discussion I drew on Staiger's notion of 'performative authorship', in which she advanced the case that, where appropriate to understandings of the shared history of non-dominant groups 'authorship has great potential' and was prepared in these cases to pardon certain 'cautions' that arise in the pursuit of 'citation [...] practices' (Staiger 2003: 52). Yet to pardon certain authors and not others is, in my view, to re-enable auteurist hierarchies and to allow identity determinisms in the interpretation only of selected films.

It would be counter to my own goals to dispute the principle that, through actual and ideological exchanges between producer and receiver, authorship can bring about pleasures through identity associations. I think it is more inclusive, though, to see the modern author as a route to pleasure, which is available to groups other than marginalised communities and the educated middle classes (not the same thing as saying that the author is not a reading preference within such groups). I have also sided with two attitudes that are worth re-establishing if we are to engage in potential modifications of a history of authored films. The first is that our analysis should begin not with modes of reception at all but with modes of production. *INLAND EMPIRE* and *Mulholland Dr.*, for example, are quite different texts, especially in respect of their modes of production and marketing, despite sometimes being read publically as companion pieces. The second is the idea that we view modern auteurs as manifest rather than concealed; as humanist horizons of expectation functioning in the same way as generic horizons do. In order to get a feel for how the modern auteur functions, in other words, we need, as I have said, to locate his or her presence in all phases of the industrial process.

I have already shown in this book that authorial speculations are fundamentally erroneous, but this should not mean that they are any less valuable in understanding how the author functions in the pleasure of film consumption. Equally, genre criticism is beset with its own limitations. We know that generic categorisation is intrinsic to film organisation and reception, but the assumption that generic categories are inflexible is a reductive business just as much as auteurism is a speculative one. As Andrew Tudor (1974: 135) remarked in *Theories of Film*:

To take a genre such as the 'western', analyse it, and list its principle characteristics is to beg the question that we must first isolate the body of films which are 'westerns'. But they can only be isolated on the basis of the 'principle characteristics', which can only be discovered from the films themselves after they have been isolated.

My intention in this final chapter is to show that *Mulholland Dr.* is not, under the historical divide between the two concepts, *essentially* auteurist any more than it is *essentially* generic. This idea echoes, I think, Bazin's sentiment (as touched upon and ultimately dismissed by Wollen) that the auteur might be better thought of as generic artist if, that is, we choose to think of the auteur as an artist at all. I believe we are better served to historical ends if we understand texts through their component parts that vie for domination – and not exclusivity – in the audience's consciousness.

This proposition carries strong reverberations of Barthes's (1981: 211) belief that we understand texts as vessels, which invite 'a tissue of quotations drawn from the innumerable centres of culture'. In backing Barthes's general premise, I have attached importance to the proposition that a reader/writer will bring together any individual combination of generic and humanist expectations in their encounter with our final example, *Mulholland Dr.* But in trying to understand how *Mulholland Dr.* raises reception questions other than *just* authorial questions, the very problem Barthes helped us bypass, that of the paradigmatic reader, presents difficulties for our historical undertaking. We can, after all, only make valid claims for a textual historicity if we start to isolate some of those 'innumerable centres of culture' even if this enterprise does work to 'reduce the plurality of entrances' (Barthes 1975b: 5) that a post-structural reading paradigm would open up. In fact, I think it is valid to view the kinds of texts and ephemera under analysis in this book as textual features in themselves; expansions of individual films rather than sovereign intertexts.

But there is a still more fundamental issue at stake. Typically, and while I am tolerant of the suggestion that it is not unthinkable that a Lynch film could be happened upon (and even then institutional contexts may play their part), spectators are discerning in their consumptions and will have first pulled to one side the drapes of promotion, publicity and criticism in order to reveal an animate text of the kinds Barthes described. Only then will she or he pass individual judgement on that text and on how accurately it was conveyed to them previously (or, for that matter, subsequently).

These sources, in effect 'textual spokespersons', are themselves ephemeral and multifarious.

Nevertheless, this chapter is the culmination of research that has shown that reception enclaves thrive and, while within those enclaves there is room for differences of opinion, there are yardsticks for what constitutes a Lynch film, an auteur picture or a genre picture; and for what counts as authenticity and what counts as fraud; and for what passes and what does not pass as satisfying cinema. There is a criterion for sexual attractiveness and there is, in the final outcome, the letter of moral law that binds us as a modern Western culture in the first place. In this respect, the audience works for meaning within the limits of language in the same way that producers do. If this were not the case, then there would be no call for the types of artefacts I have been dealing with in this book to begin with.

Authors and Industry

Through the example of *Twin Peaks*, we saw how Lynch became a utility in the reception of prime-time television drama. It was, in fact, ABC's[2] attempts to create a new television event that led to the production of *Mulholland Dr.* as a pilot film for a possible television series in the first place. The fact, though, that *Mulholland Dr.* was eventually realised as a cinematic feature was the upshot of absorbing struggles between the interests of the artist and the industry. Indeed, by reflecting upon *Mulholland Dr.*'s production history, we are shown some insight into the ways in which the authored text is an abstract, unformulated concept that accommodates commercial needs according, in this example, to overlapping industrial (televisual and cinematic) and geographical (North American and European) contexts.

In taking up this idea I want to draw upon an article entitled 'Creative differences' published over two issues of *New Yorker* in August/September 1999, in which Tad Friend chronicled the creative and commercial struggles between Lynch and the ABC executives. In his transcript Friend draws upon interviews with some of the strategic players involved in the pre-production and production of the *Mulholland Dr.* pilot.

Friend describes how the ABC network became interested in the prospect of a show that would 'be both a critical and a popular success'; a show that 'wouldn't be just another knockoff of [the popular situation comedy] "Friends". Steve Tao, ABC's Vice President of drama programming, explained how 'Just the title alone had us really excited ... "David Lynch's 'Mulholland Drive'!". Faced with the 'plethora of sameness on TV', Tao believed that 'David Lynch's television [stood] out' and was persuaded by the argument that 'a show by [Lynch] could be one of those large events [...] that people gather together to watch'. ABC was 'trying to create appointment television'. On this point Friend quotes Don Ohlmeyer, a retired president of the NBC network, who had maintained that 'for a show to be a breakout hit, there has to be some magic that happens with the audience' even if 'nobody knows what that is'. From an industrial perspective, then, Lynch's name (which following the release of *Lost Highway* and *The Straight Story* had recouped much of its cultural cachet) might be re-harnessed to offer the horizonal promise of a show that could be simultaneously popular, captivating and different.

Friend provides a transcript of the *Mulholland Dr.* pitch that Lynch and his 'production partner' Tony Krantz presented to a panel of ABC network executives. Friend noted that it (the pitch) 'was unusual not just because it was tantalizingly brief but because Lynch was so candid about his intention to do something sui generis'. The pitch, in fact, only described generic (mystery) elements of the project:

Exterior night – Hollywood Hills, Los Angeles. Darkness. Distant sounds of freeway traffic. Then the closer sound of a car – its headlights illuminate an oleander bush and the limbs of a eucalyptus tree. Then the headlights turn – a street sign is suddenly brightly lit. The words of the sign read 'Mulholland Drive.' The car moves under the sign as it turns and the words fall once again into darkness [...] the black Cadillac limousine pulls over and the driver points a gun at the beautiful brunette in the back seat. Just then, two cars [full] of drag racing teenagers scream around the corner, and one car slams into the limo. The woman staggers out of the wreck and, severely dazed, makes her way down hill toward Hollywood.

[...] The brunette from the limo, Rita, makes her way to an apartment complex carrying only a purse containing a hundred and twenty-five thousand dollars in cash and a blue key. Stricken with amnesia, she is befriended by a quirky blonde, Betty, who has just arrived from Canada and is determined to become a movie star. Betty tries to help Rita figure out who she is – even as the police, and Rita's less kindly pursuers, begin looking for her. (Friend 1999)

Referring to this outline as 'the best kind of pitch, where you're on the edge of your seat', Tao, spoke of 'the creepiness of this woman in this horrible, horrible crash, and [Lynch] teasing us with the notion that people are chasing her. She's not just "in" trouble – she is trouble. Obviously we asked, what happens next? And [Lynch] said, "you have to buy the pitch for me to tell you". And so on the strength of this, ABC did buy the pitch.

Friend recounts that 'ABC was so eager to sign Lynch that it promptly put up four and a half million dollars for […] a two-hour pilot'. In addition, the Disney-owned Touchstone Television contributed a further 'two and a half million more, for a total budget of seven million, with the proviso – which Lynch grudgingly accepted – that he shoot extra footage to be used as a "closed ending"' on the agreement that 'Disney's Buena Vista International intended to recoup the company's money by releasing a longer version as a film in Europe'. (We may recall that the pilot show for Twin Peaks was released as a freestanding feature in Europe.)

Despite the horizonal lure of Lynch, which promised his take on what Friend called the type of television 'bewilderment' that 'American viewers relished' – and which had been only recently evidenced through the popularity of 'offbeat television shows [such] as "Northern Exposure" and "The X-Files"' – ABC became 'hooked on the generic elements of a mystery thriller whose enigmas might be fleshed out over one or more series'. Friend reports that creative and commercial tensions occurred only when Lynch presented a 92-page script for the pilot; the point at which some of the more Lynchian elements of Mulholland Dr. came to notice. As Friend tells it, ABC executives began to 'wonder how seemingly unconnected scenes and characters would be tied together' and there were mumblings that Lynch's script, 'dense with dream images', did not 'gather up loose ends and sweep to a close'. Through Tao once more, Friend reports that although Mulholland Dr.'s 'strangeness' was conceived as a selling point 'it was also a cause for concern' given the 'very fine balance between intriguing people and confusing people'. So concerned, in fact, were ABC about the over-encroaching Lynchian elements of the script that two weeks after receiving the script ABC 'summoned about twenty people from the network […] and Lynch's production company to meet in ABC's conference room'. As Friend said:

> At 'notes meetings' like this one, networks begin to put their stamp on a show, analyzing everything from the characters' morals to their hairstyles. Executives try to clarify motivations and future plot lines: 'What is at stake?

What is the character's arc? [...] Will there be a love story, a combative mating dance?' Most executives believe that television shows – unlike movies which people actively seek out – are watched passively by a tired and fickle audience; and so stories should move quickly and clearly, and character' problems should engender immediate sympathy. (1999)

According to Friend, ABC executives worked on the premise that 'to achieve popular success with an artist' one needed to 'take whatever it is that makes that artist distinctive, dilute it, and add a spoonful of sugar'. On this point Brian Grazer, a co-chairman of ABC's Imagine Television company (and producers for *Mulholland Dr.*), offered the view that 'television should bring out the best in David [Lynch]' not because his films bucked the system – 'become too original as he [Lynch] has sometimes done [and] you go south' – but 'because people want originality within a conventional format'. Indeed, once Lynch had begun to submit daily rushes the 'time-honored pattern of antagonism between the "talent" and the "suits"' set in and brought about an ideological standoff whereby, in Tao's words 'executives view writers as unruly teen-agers' and 'writers see executives as hysterical parents who, regrettably, still control allowances and bedtimes' (Friend 1999).

Friend proceeds to describe how ABC executives became anxious over the film's pacing, which was considered a 'bit plodding', and the casting of the two female leads who, according to Tao, were 'fantastic-looking, fine talents, but a little old – both are in their late 20s – and ABC thinks Betty is too aw-shucks' while Rita 'looks kind of goofy'. The feeling was that Lynch had been given too much latitude and that ABC had deferred to him without having seen the actors read. More detailed concerns were communicated through ABC's Standards and Practices department, whose function it is to vet ABC shows for 'objectionable material'. Friend reports on the 'ream of memos' that were sent out to Lynch by the department suggesting a number of modifications. The department objected to some of the language used in the film: 'butts and boobs', for instance, should replace 'tits and ass'. Nor should we be shown a 'hit-man's gun "blowing brains across desk, carpet and walls"', or, a bullet 'hitting a fat woman's buttocks'. Lynch was even asked to 'lose' a close shot of 'dog turds on a sidewalk' to which he took particular objection, but agreed finally on a compromise where the 'poop would take up only one eighth of the screen'. And the Standards and Practices people were 'particularly concerned by Lynch's reverence for cigarettes [and] for smoke and fire as a magical texture' because, as Tao protested 'we don't condone smoking here at the network'. So once more a compromise was reached. As Friend reports (through Tao), Lynch 'found ways around it, now it's mostly the bad people who smoke…you smoke you die'. Indeed the network was insistent that characters that smoke should manifest 'a hacking cough'. Lynch did in fact change the script so that it is Adam (Justin Theroux), and not a sympathetic landlady who lights up, but in a scene filmed after the network delivered its diktat, Friend reports how Lynch directed Theroux to 'Take a really fucking big drag – fucking love that cigarette' (1999).

Given ABC's reservations about *Mulholland Dr.*'s slow pacing (amongst other things), the proposition seemed likely for a time that the pilot would, against vehement opposition from Lynch (according to Friend, Lynch had pushed to have it run at two and a half hours), be aired at a cut down 88 minutes. Although Lynch eventually toed the network line, cutting the running time for the reason that, while he now viewed the pilot as a 'sick little garden', he would 'rather lose seeds than the whole series' (which at this time was still a possibility). Krantz was left to lament that the edited pilot was more like television but 'paradoxically, less necessary as television. What had distinguished it' he surmised 'had gone […] *Mulholland Drive* was no longer what ABC had gambled on' (Friend 1999).

Friend's article leads us finally to May 1999 when ABC, like other networks, made its annual presentations of its fall prime-time schedules to advertising agencies. The network had initially planned to woo advertisers by using *Mulholland Dr.* as a vehicle for lowering the median age of the network's viewers – which 'at forty-one […] was well above the coveted demographic of eighteen to thirty-four'. In the event, ABC chose to go instead with a show called *Wasteland* while *Mulholland Dr.* was sidelined for re-editing into a mid-season, two-hour TV movie, the prospect of which Lynch likened to 'an accident […] a sad, bad traffic accident' (Friend 1999).

Friend's transcript reveals the divergence of interests at work in the creation of the filmic text (although, as we shall see the author might be granted greater freedoms within the dedicated context of post-classical art cinema). Yet if we return to Wollen for a moment, we can see that he too draws his conclusions from transcripts of Curtiz's struggles within the system. Indeed, we will recollect that Wollen lauded Curtiz on the grounds of his ability to get his own way by means of 'his prestige, obstinacy, negotiating skills, or [his] capacity for intimidation' (Wollen 2003: 70).

How, then, might we read the inclusion, say, of the compromised, not-so-close shot of dog turds on a sidewalk in *Mulholland Dr.*? Presumably, given the rationale on which his defence of Curtiz is based, Wollen would back this gesture as an auteurist intervention and would characterise Lynch's determination to save a shot that might have a signature function but no narrational properties, as a compromise between feuding parties. One might be led to ask: does all this really have any bearing? Because if we are to choose to see the author and the system as co-dependents it surely should not matter at all. The possibility of an auteurist reading of this single shot (albeit as indicative of the film more widely) is no more than a receptive preference in the end. We can pursue this line of thought through an analysis of *Mulholland Dr.*'s promotion and reception, where we can show that the film's horizonal signs are not fixed but are instead impressionable according to given contexts. In other words, films might or might not, or might to one degree or other, flaunt their poetic characteristics.

Selling *Mulholland Dr.*

We know that Lynch has occupied a prominent position within an aesthetically dispersed post-classical system, wherein he has been able to work under much greater freedoms than his classical predecessors (e.g. Curtiz). Part of the conflict between Lynch and ABC came about because the network ultimately retained studio-like control over the final cut for *Mulholland Dr.* and, of course, it dictated absolutely exhibition strategies. But as we now know, Lynch's fortunes were to change. In March 2000 the French entertainment conglomerate CanalPlus bid $7m for the *Mulholland Dr.* pilot while supplying a further $2m of funding for Lynch to complete a new ending for a freestanding theatrical feature. Indeed, Mary Sweeney, Lynch's long-time collaborator and editor on *Mulholland Dr.*, was filled with enthusiasm for the finished film that was in her view 'completely fantastic and much more like David's usual thing'. In the same breath Sweeney spoke of the film's generic attributes: 'its entertainment value is pretty darn high…It's really sexy; the girls are gorgeous; the guys are handsome; it's Hollywood and it's fun' (Hughes 2002: 240). What Sweeney is describing in rudiment is a post-classical film, much like any other post-classical film in generic respect, in that it is composed through a series of

Mulholland Dr. promotional poster.

textual and extra-textual relationships. There is nothing new in this proposition, of course, but we can make more robust claims on a textual historicity if we welcome into our equation the ephemera that these days play such a principal part in the practices of film consumption.

A signed text hints at a deferential filmic pedigree, and sustained by the promotional methods of the industry, horizonal expectations will be set for the knowledgeable cineaste who will be able to speculate upon the film's textual features. In the critical reception of films meanwhile, the auteur is defined as such through his or her reflective understanding of generic conventions and the ability to rework them in new contexts. Understood this way the auteur is fundamentally a genre artist. This point has a historical basis and, as Wollen pointed out, goes back to the earliest debates between Bazin and the other *Cahiers* critics. But what comes to light in this analysis is that the post-classical text must, in the service of commerce, be simultaneously generic (objective) and auteurist (subjective) in the customary use of the terms.

There is a widely held belief (certainly amongst Europeans) that the art movie is less agreeable to American audiences and more to the liking of refined European tastes. It is an assumption borne out in promotional campaigns for *Mulholland Dr.* As the production history of the film showed us, it was always the intention to release *Mulholland Dr.* as a dedicated feature in Europe even before CanalPlus came to the project's rescue. But what we can see through a comparative account of the dedicated trailers (US (Universal) and European (StudioCanal)) is that in both contexts horizonal paradigms are organised around generic and, to a lesser extent, subject intertexts, although such an emphasis will be variable depending on the degree of stardom or notoriety of the subjects in other films.

The American theatrical trailer[3] begins by establishing the film's opening enigma. We hear a hushed conversation between two women: 'What happened?' 'It was an accident', comes the reply. At this point we fade up from black to the film's violent night-time head-on car crash. Now we are introduced through close shot to the first of the two female leads, Rita (Laura Elena Harring), who locates the dialogue, saying: 'a car accident'. Shortly after the showing of industry logos and the film's title, we are introduced to our second protagonist, a bright-eyed Betty (Naomi Watts) who steps out of a taxi and gazes in jaw-dropped wonder at her new surroundings. We now dissolve to an iconic panoramic shot of LA at night (which we may or may not recognise as the view from Mulholland Drive) while the text... 'A WOMAN IN SEARCH OF STARDOM' is superimposed.

Even under the historical guide of horizonal expectations, and even in the context of post-classical cinema where the promotional and critical mechanisms are fully matured, we still need to keep in mind the problem of the paradigmatic reader. I will come to this point in due course, but suffice to say here that, although a cast of relatively unknown actors (at that point in their careers anyway) performed *Mulholland Dr.*, it is possible that Harring and Watts (who, as the film's protagonists, will dominate both trailers' shot ratios) and the other actors might figure as subject intertexts in the formation of horizonal expectations. Indeed, biographies of actors and other talents (including the director in most examples) are, nowadays, familiar features on official websites, DVDs and other related media[4] and might even offer a route to new horizons for the more concentrated cineaste. Having said that, at a more universal level, the 'gorgeous girls' referred to by Sweeney function in the American and European trailers, as they do in the film, as object intertexts. Betty and Rita, it must be acknowledged, feature as causal agents in the film's narrative; but, within the scope of the classical cinematic paradigm, Betty and Rita also provide scopophilic pleasures.

The details of such shooting strategies hardly need to be reviewed here. Suffice to say that in both American and European trailers the stars' eroticism is routinely emphasised through an emphasis on fetishistic framing strategies (the close shot predominantly). Yet if we have seen *Mulholland Dr.* (and trailers are typically directed at those who have not) we will know that as the film's narrative develops, Rita and Betty become emotionally and romantically entangled (lovers indeed). This is a decisive plot development, since Rita's ultimate rejection of Betty results in Betty's emotional and physical disintegration leading, ultimately, to her suicide. It is here that we can begin to trace a divergence of apparent cultural preferences through the two trailers.

The American trailer makes no explicit or implicit reference to Rita and Betty's sexual relationship. The trailer, in fact, dupes us by implying that the narrative might follow the boy-meets-girl-gets-girl conventions of the classical Oedipal saga. This is achieved through the juxtaposition of two abstract shots. The first connects us to the previous shot of Betty emerging from the taxi. We see her in close shot (and still awestruck) as she announces, 'I just came here from Deep River Ontario and now I'm in this dream place'. This shot is juxtaposed with an interior shot of Adam who is shown with headphones, sat in a director's chair and whose fixed attention is drawn to an off-screen presence: Betty, we might assume since we will associate the two shots and we also know by now that Betty is a would-be actress because of the earlier shot of LA and the text that tells us the film is about 'a woman in search of stardom'. Because our horizonal expectations for classical storytelling will predict the development of heterosexual relationships, a logical association is made between Betty and Adam even though an emotional relationship between the two never materialises.

Both trailers play on the conventions of the mystery thriller. But unlike its American counterpart, the European trailer hints much more at a same-sex erotic thriller by emphasising the emotionally ruinous sexual relationship between Betty and Rita who, in terms of a Lynchian subject intertext, perform an act of splitting and doubling since they may also be called respectively Diane and Camilla. The European trailer features shots of Betty and Rita/Camilla lying in bed together. In another shot they are kissing, in another leaning together in tears, foreheads touching. A close shot shows Rita/Camilla looking alluringly off screen as we hear Betty's off-screen whisper, 'Camilla, you've come back'. The European trailer also shows a shot of Betty that disobeys the erotic demands of classical spectatorship. In this example we are shown a dishevelled Betty sat in a diner, in a state of obvious distress, and presented as ashen and gaunt, without make up and wearing a discoloured and stained white vest. In fact, she is barely recognisable as the same character and a very long way removed from the picture of eroticism used in wider promotion of the film.

I shall return to the erotic element of *Mulholland Dr.*, but here the promotion of *Mulholland Dr.* as conservative (American) and progressive (European) texts can be explored more thoroughly through the different, if overlapping, leanings on object and subject intertexts. In addition to predominant shots of the players, there is consistency across both trailers in that they share similar geographic iconography. Shots of LA, the Hollywood Hills, the Mulholland Drive road sign add up to establish the film's temporal and spatial milieu. Likewise, both trailers emphasise the mystery-LA-noir elements of the film. The American trailer, for instance, connects the shots of plain-clothed detectives at a crime scene (one cogitating 'could be someone's missing') with a chiaroscuro extreme close shot of a man's lips (as if speaking into a phone although we cannot see a receiver) saying 'the girl is missing' (the expressionistic and claustrophobic framing of the latter shot is most conventionally noirish). In terms of its object intertexts, the horizontal offer of both trailers suggests a LA noir-thriller should we pre-imagine such a thing.

But unlike its European counterpart, the American trailer also offers the promise of American cultural nostalgia with the inclusion of images of jitterbugging couples accompanied by a soundtrack with a rock 'n' roll ballad (these images are in fact taken from the film's opening credit titles). But, perhaps more telling in terms of object and subject intertexts is the service of a voice-over and the explicit citation of Lynch's name in the promotions of the film. Referring to the latter, firstly, the American trailer shows us title credits, telling us that *Mulholland Dr.* is 'From David Lynch, the director of *Twin Peaks* and *Blue Velvet*' and we are shown the 'Best Director Cannes Film Festival 2001 laurel', which Lynch was awarded in recognition of the film. Here we even cut to a potential subject intertext in the shape of the signature motif of a faulty flickering electric light bulb. Indeed, this shot is so abstract (in the context of the trailer) that its inclusion would appear *only* to act to trigger a subject association.

We might think that the above strategies hold the potential to alienate the wider public since Lynch would be considered to be something of an acquired taste. But other than as a knowing subject intertext the shot of the light bulb is rather inconsequential. It is fleeting and, perhaps, mysterious, but it does not hold the power to override or even interfere with the trailer's more familiar object intertexts. Similarly, the citation of Lynch's name will also have the potential to alienate audiences (as well as entice them). But at the same time Lynch's name might function as an object intertext in the sense that horizonal expectations of a Lynch text are not necessarily dependent upon privileged subject knowledge. It can be the fact that the film is an authored work at all that marks its pedigree as a cinematic artwork.

We are also reminded that David Lynch is the director of *Blue Velvet* and *Twin Peaks*, and that, as well as being Lynch's most famous and acclaimed works, they also lean towards the more open aspects of his textual spectrum. But even if we do recall the more conceptual elements of these works, the trailer acts to promote *Mulholland Dr.*'s generic horizons through its heavy emphasis on object intertexts which are further (if erroneously) stabilised through the inclusion of a voice-over. We have already established that object intertexts confirm for us that this is a melodrama and a mystery LA noir. But in addition to the shots I have already described, we see further thematic confirmations of a mystery in shots of Rita sobbing, 'I don't know who I am' and Betty, with reference to a large wad of $100 bills in Rita's purse, asking, 'That money? You don't know where it came from'?

The classical realist text will accommodate enigmas but on the proviso that those enigmas be solved come the end of the film at the latest. And, as we may also know, a Lynchian text will happily embrace open-ended narratives. In this sense, *Mulholland Dr.* meets typical subject horizons since many of *Mulholland Dr.'s* enigmas are left unresolved. But the American trailer implies that the mystery will in fact be solved and so the film will service demands for resolution and closure. So as the trailer proceeds we hear an exchange between Rita and Betty:

> 'I remember something'…
> 'What is it Rita?'…
> 'Mulholland Drive'…
> 'Mulholland Drive?'…
> 'That's where I was going'.

Meanwhile, and stretched over the duration of the trailer, a voice-over implies closure:

> 'A woman in search of herself'…
> 'in the city of dreams'…
> 'the key to a mystery'…
> 'lies somewhere' …
> 'on Mulholland Drive'.

As I have indicated already, the European trailer operates through similar object intertexts but is at variance in other ways. Firstly, the StudioCanal trailer makes no reference to Lynch by name (although we might recall that StudioCanal did banner *Mulholland Dr.* on its website as 'A contemporary film noir, directed by David Lynch' (www.studiocanal.com/ movie/mulhollanddrive). which is itself minor vindication of the points I am making here). Nor is there any use of a voice-over to aid or imply narrative comprehension. One can only speculate upon the exclusion of Lynch's name. I wonder if in this instance Lynch could be perceived as a commercially disadvantageous intertext, especially as the trailer offers a poetic paradigm anyway (after all, those in the know or Lynch enthusiasts would probably be aware of the film's authorship already through related media channels).

The StudioCanal trailer features shots that are inexplicable outside the context of the film (or possibly even within the context of the film). We see a brief exchange between two men in a diner in which the first says, 'I had a dream about this place' as the other urges 'Tell me'. The trailer also features an enigmatic tableau of a man in a suit standing on a stage who, in an exaggerated theatrical gesture and while skilfully spinning a cane through his fingers, shouts out in a first-person address (and this despite the presence of a microphone stand in the middle foreground) 'there is no band, and yet... we hear a band'. We are shown, too, an unfathomable close shot of a monstrous, scorched-looking face with rotten teeth and blood-red eyes. These shots compete with and upset the otherwise harmonious object intertexts that promise, in the broadest generic terms, a contemporary LA noir.

The auteurist might know that Lynch's authorship is partly written in terms of oblique dream worlds and demons so shots such as these might well operate as subject intertexts. But they operate simultaneously at a level of object intertext too. Our horizontal expectations might be shaped through a foreknowledge of the Lynchian text, as they will be for the auteurist critic, but in wider circles of reception it is more probable – more desirable, even, from a commercial perspective – that they will not. Shots like these, then, will function as object intertexts that connote something uniquely anterior (i.e. above and beyond the acceptable permits of generic innovation) to the usual generic expectations; a text of poetic character in other words.

Receiving *Mulholland Dr.*

The intersecting industrial systems of modern film production and reception present us with a set of author propositions a long way removed from those of the haughty literary establishment of 1960s to which Barthes and Foucault took exception. We are no longer dependent only on scholarship to conquer the text on our behalf because early auteurism has come to the fore in public criticism, while the author's name is now an ally of commerce. Meanwhile, a defining feature of the post-classical system, is its adaptability in feeding niche audiences; and this feature communicates, as we shall now see, with those audiences through various populist and serious media channels that will reference the author's name when and where that reference seems fitting. So given that the auteur has become a regular feature in the day-to-day consumption of films, it would in my view be negligent to overlook promotional and critical influences upon horizonal expectations for post-classical films.

With this in mind, I want to turn my attention towards Lynch's authorship in respect of the promotion and reception of *Mulholland Dr.* As I have said, it has become routine for post-classical auteurs to feature in publicity for their films and in this respect they can become public figures, or even star auteurs. Indeed the public profile of a director can, as it has done in Lynch's case, reach beyond the restrictions of specialist film journalism and literature and even in vast public arenas directors can command relatively high profiles although the nature of the film will determine the context for their publicity.

Lynch was a guest, for instance, on the NBC network's prime-time *The Tonight Show* hosted by Jay Leno on 31 October 2001. It is not the business of light entertainment shows such as these to offer earnest exegesis, so while Lynch takes his typical stance in refusing to account for the film's 'open endedness' – 'film is its own language … it's a horrible shame to translate that language back into words' – Leno, while admitting that he did not understand the film but that he 'really liked it' and 'would watch it again', wanted to know about more irreverent issues such as the pattern for Lynch's vacations, whether he is a 'beach guy', and his relationships with his actresses.

The interview features an excerpt from the film in which Adam is shown directing a scene for his own film in which an unnamed male actor is showing difficulty in kissing Camilla (Rita) with the appropriate ardour. Adam demonstrates how he wants the actor to perform by taking Camilla in his own arms and kissing her. The scene hints at a conflict of professional and personal interests as Adam orders the set to be cleared and the lights dimmed as he and Camilla become engrossed in their clinch. Camilla, meanwhile, has asked for Diane (Betty) to be allowed to stay on the set and we see her in a state of emotional torment as she looks on longingly at the two lovers. We know that in *Mulholland Dr.* Diane and Camilla are lovers and by placing the scene in the wider context of the film we will recognise that Camilla is manipulating Diane's emotional suffering. But abstracted in this way, the scene connotes very different meanings and serves, like Universal's trailer before it, wider promotional functions.

On the one hand, the scene illustrates a film director at work and having shown it, Leno asks Lynch 'have you done that? Is it a little bit autobiographical?' to which Lynch playfully replies 'with all the girls, it sometimes can happen'. Leno persists 'it sometimes can happen?' at which point Lynch retracts 'I wish, yeah'. On the other, the excerpt functions in the same way as the film's American trailer in the sense that there is nothing to denote that there is anything else than a heterosexual love triangle at play. While Leno stresses that *Mulholland Dr.* will appeal 'if you like to think when you go to the movies and like to figure things out', and secures Lynch as a subject intertext by introducing him as the 'Oscar nominated director who's works include *Blue Velvet*, *Twin Peaks* [and] my favourite, *The Straight Story*', emphasis is placed on the film's object intertexts since Watts and Harring, neither of whom are referred to by name, indicate an erotic temptation.

> *Leno*: 'The movie has some very sexy scenes.'
> *Lynch*: 'You liked those scenes Jay?'
> *Leno*: 'It was very good. The two girls were terrific.'
> *Lynch*: 'Fantastic.'
> *Leno* (closing the interview): 'It's not for dumb people. It's an interesting movie, and very, very, sexy. You have some very sexy scenes in there. It's called *Mulholland Drive*, it's in theatres right now. David Lynch. David, thank you very much.'[5]

Like promotion and criticism, publicity is compliant to context and emphasis on meaning will be shaded accordingly. So broad appeal publications such as *Entertainment Weekly* might stress the textual (erotic) appeal of the stars, but not to the exclusion of other intertexts. In a studio-posed image that occupies the same amount of copy as the text, Watts is introduced to the reader as the 'Best Schizo Sweetie' and we are told that 'as Betty, Mulholland Drive's bright-eyed, bipolar non-genue, Watts more than stood her ground at stage center of David Lynch's swirling psychological kaleidoscope' (Brown 2001). *Premiere*, meanwhile, carried an article 'Twin piques' that featured sexually suggestive full-body images of Watts and Harring under the title 'LYNCHPINUPS' while the caption extended the sexual innuendo … 'Naomi Watts and Laura Elena Harring arouse curiosity, among other things, in David Lynch's Mulholland Drive'. Although the article is organised around comments attributed to both actors (to the exclusion of Lynch), Lynch retains his agency even in this re-ordering of the confluence of object and subject signs. This is made clear in the article's opening paragraph:

> With *Mulholland Drive*, David Lynch has left the straight stories and lawnmowers behind, and embraced those symbols that his fans would surely tell him are truly Lynchian: twisted dreams, midgets, and stunning performances by gorgeous girls you probably haven't heard of until now. (David 2001)

It scarcely needs reaffirming here that Lynch's name will be omnipresent in reviews. Scrutiny of such reviews will reveal an implicit understanding of the auteur as a genre artist and of film as an amalgam of subject and object intertexts of which any combination will constitute individual horizonal paradigms. But Lynch is the all-pervading feature that, to one degree or other, informs across all these assessments.

So for the likes of Graham Fuller (2001), *Mulholland Dr.* was a 'lethally perfumed neo-noir' that deploys a 'Chandlerian use of LA's iconic topography' and an 'ambient postmodern Hollywood gothic' while in Diane we were given a 'winning amalgam of Doris Day and Grace Kelly'. For Tom Charity (2002) the film was not only 'a neo-*noir* mystery thriller, but [...] also a surreal comedy – a Hollywood outsider satire – and a romantic nightmare'. Manohla Dargis (2001) summarised the film as 'a first-rate horror movie about one girl's once-upon-a-time in Hollywood and her unhappily ever after' while Glen Kenny (2001) commented on the film's 'menacingly polite cowboy who looks as if he just stepped out of an establishing shot from a Republic Pictures B western'.

What we are pointed towards in these examples is the seemingly unbounded range of object intertexts that can come into play in the reconstruction of a given film. And while there is room for some generic overlap these critics are, in a manner of speaking, describing different films. But Lynch's sign – the film's Lynchian intertexts – comes to dictate across all these readings. Fuller (2001) talked, for instance, of a 'Magrittian surrealism [that] has an erotic morbidity that only an appreciator of the limits of decadence such as Lynch could pull off' and like 'Hitchcock's *Vertigo*, Bergman's *Persona* and Buñuel's *That Obscure Object of Desire*' Lynch breaks 'through the dream fabric of the film, reminding us of the fragility of cinema's hallucinatory power'. Charity's (2002) feeling was that 'David Lynch doesn't make movies like other people. He concocts moods.

Colours. Flavours', and *Mulholland Dr.* ranked as a 'sinister and seductive masterwork'. Dargis (2001) thought the film was typically Lynchian 'doppelgangers come and go, identities shift, as do time and space, hot girls and hair color. It would be easy to suggest that Lynch is merely hauling out his hoary preoccupations', while Kenny (2001) set to the task of pinpointing the 'nonstop catalogue of classic Lynchian moments'. But where does all this leave us, finally, in respect of understanding the pleasures in the recognition of the author sign and how can this textual pleasure tally with the recording of a film history? In thinking about these questions we come back one last time to the rivalry between authorial and generic analysis and, in the light of this standoff, the relationship between the critic and the public.

What the politique did was to bring about the potential for a reclassification of certain Hollywood films. But, inadvertently perhaps, the politique established a critical inheritance that turned in on itself by presenting new textual hierarchies. Bazin (1981: 46), as we know, preferred not to single out 'the talent of this or that film-maker' but championed instead 'the genius of the system'. Even so, the classical Hollywood film still allowed him to espouse the honourable virtues of 'social truth' and its attendant textual and thematic realisms. True to Bazin's word, the system has consolidated its genius – its 'vigorous tradition and its fertility when it comes into contact with new elements' (that includes its commercial ingestion of the auteur) – even if not always, or, indeed, often, to the ends of social self-awareness that Bazin would have preferred.

Barthes seemed to help us overcome these hierarchal dilemmas in his rallying call for the individual hermeneutic rights of the reader that insisted upon the institutional author's death. But even Barthes's reading paradigms were built on the understanding that modern (writerly) texts rank above their realist (readerly) counterparts. But I believe it amounts to something of an equivocation to endlessly defer on meaning because we must not suppose a paradigmatic reader. To do this is to overlook the myriad competing subject and object intertexts that make up horizontal paradigms and construe our individual and shared horizons of expectations for post-classical art cinema. Our consumption of films is not usually an arbitrary business after all.

Hierarchal textual decorums have tested theorists and historians predating Bazin, Barthes, the *Cahiers* group and the like. In his influential

1936 essay 'The work of art in the age of mechanical reproduction', Walter Benjamin championed the possibility of a progressive popular cinema on the grounds that by diminishing the aura of the artwork (through mechanical reproduction) we might eradicate the need for the critic in the first place and thus make way for an 'art of the proletariat'. Benjamin (1973: 212–27), who seems less far removed from Bazin in his admiration of Hollywood, went so far as to suggest that in the 'art of a classless society' concepts of 'creativity and genius, eternal value and mystery' would become 'outmoded'. Indeed the 'greater the decrease in the social significance of an art form', he concluded 'the sharper the distinction between criticism and enjoyment by the public'.

But Benjamin did not envision a modern Hollywood system wherein classical texts compete with or overlap modernist ones. In addition to its more traditional readerly textual pleasures, then, contemporary Hollywood now offers the predisposed reader/writer the potential for more blissful pleasures to be fulfilled too. What Benjamin was not able to predict was Hollywood's adaptability; its readiness to manufacture texts that allowed for ideas of 'creativity ... genius, eternal value and mystery' to be written into them. Hollywood may well remain the 'art of a classless society'. But it is through the figure of author that we can make more substantiated claims for a diminishing 'distinction between criticism and enjoyment by the public'; that is, a critical enjoyment that will emerge in the writerly textual pleasures that the real and the imagined author proffers.

Conclusion

In a feature published in 2003 (not long after the release of *Mulholland Dr.*), *The Guardian* newspaper asked a panel of experts to draw up a league table of the 40 most internationally important working directors. The article reported that, 'no one could fault the conclusion that David Lynch is the most important film-maker of the current era' and Lynch duly topped the table (beating Martin Scorsese into second place by a single point). Lynch was graded (out of 20): '17 for substance, 18 for look, 18 for craft, 19 for originality' and '17 for intelligence'. Lynch achieved this distinction, moreover, because his films seemed to offer, 'a portal into the collective subconscious' and because, 'the daydream notion conjured up in tales such as *Blue Velvet*, *Lost Highway* or *Mulholland Drive* is by turn frightening exasperating, revelatory and wild'. The panel concluded that; 'nobody makes films like David Lynch' (reprinted at Film.guardian.co.uk/features/page/0,11456,1082823.00.html 22.12.2003).

This example does nothing to dissuade us from the view that auteurism is hierarchal and partisan. At the same time, *The Guardian*'s poll only reflects our continuing fascination with the figure of the auteur and the pleasure she or he can bring in the everyday consumption of films. And it comes as no surprise to us in our daily lives when even the most levelheaded, and the most passionate, spontaneously pledge their allegiances and opinions on lists of this nature. It is this pleasure (since pleasure is a beguiling notion that might impair our best judgements) that has been too often overlooked in the requirement to sidestep the romantic pitfalls of humanism that has dogged authorship studies over recent years. Yet we have seen in the example of Lynch that so pervasive can authors be in the marketing and reception of their films that it might even seem, somewhat paradoxically perhaps, snobbishly obstinate to deny him or her a presence in the reading of the aesthetic text.

Over the course of this book I have set to the task of shedding some light on the ways in which the contemporary American auteur has become a dialogic staple in the classification and public consumption of post-classical films. In the example of Lynch, meanwhile, we have been able to see a precise demonstration of how the once discrete classical/high modernist paradigms could have dissolved, setting in place a potentially more democratic art cinema (although whether or not this amounts to any kind of utopian gesture on Hollywood's part will no doubt remain a matter of dispute). We have also seen how new Hollywood is a highly sophisticated, malleable system, amenable to the tastes of a widening audience demographic all of which posits stubborn obstacles for those apt to defend the traditions of a filmic 'outside' or, if we prefer, a filmic avant-garde. At the same time, Lynch's canonicity offers affirmations and reassurances that American films can compete for the highest international cultural rankings.

The contemporary Hollywood art film may now come with the auteur as part of its promotional baggage (and I would not be the first to historicise such a process, of course). But the author is now a more routine reading tool for a wider public audience too. This is not in itself an academic rallying call for a 'commonsensical' return to the early auteurist biotype. But the task of accounting for authorship pleasures, I believe, needs to be understood not simply through a detached a-textual historical assessment, but through an understanding of the processes of different textual consumptions too.

Through the 'death of the author' the assumption has been that the author should be expelled from the reading process since authors work against the rhythmic writerly pleasures proposed in Barthes's model for textual consumptions. Yet we have seen that author say-so, and an investment in his or her final testimony, does not regulate auteurist reading. On the contrary, imaginings of the artist and their worldviews can open up reading speculations not so very far removed from Barthes's model in the first place. Nor does the author's death lend itself to materialist history. To adopt an anti-author position is to throw the baby out with the bath water, as it were, and to simply position the radical theorist in a counter-historical binary.

And so the author struggle has delivered us at a philosophical bottleneck. We can choose either to retain the hermeneutic rights of the auteur or we can choose to dismiss him or her if it is our own agency that matters. Only a materialist history, it seems, can offer us a route away from this deadlock but then we must resist the enticements of the text. Staiger (2003: 27) noted that 'authorship does matter'. And indeed it does. But it matters not only to those marginalised groups seeking solidarities through shared histories; film authors matter to a bigger public too. Let us, then, register modern auteurism in a reception practice whereby the authored film can compete for the reader's attention in a coming together of inter- and extra-textual determinations through which the modern film spectator composes the aesthetic text for herself or himself. In this way we can respect the text and steer it clear of the divisive self-aggrandising critical hierarchies that have severed the auteurist text from the recordings of materialist film histories in the past.

Notes

Chapter 2

1   *Six Men Getting Sick* was a minute-long animated painting in which a coloured substance is shown passing through the internal organs of the figures causing them to vomit. Lynch projected the film, which he configured as a continuous loop, onto a sculptured screen (incorporating three plaster-casts of his own head), to the tape-recorded accompaniment of a siren. *The Alphabet* combined live action and animation. The four-minute film depicts a girl sitting in darkness on a bed, a plant that peppers an abstract life form with animated letters (bringing about its death) and a soundtrack featuring children chanting the alphabet.

2   The 'Eagle-Scout' ingenuousness that came to shape understandings of Lynch's films is demonstrated in his own reminiscences of this period: 'I love plumbing and carpentry. I built three sheds in my back-yard during that period. They were made out of wood that I found on my paper route. My route took me through two different trash areas. On trash nights, my route would take two hours to do instead of one because I stopped and sorted through the garbage. There are a lot of people who go through garbage, and they're not stupid people' (L'Ecuyer 1987).

3   In a filmed discussion with an unidentified (off-screen) interviewer Lynch had the following to say about independence: 'We [the industry and the artist] need each other. It's a tricky business but if you start off in the right way you have a better chance [...] you can have the same spirit in the studio [...] it's about control. It can happen in a studio with a big budget, small budget, with a production company – whatever' (Lynch 1993). (So far as I am able tell, this interview was not produced for commercial purposes. This recording is held at the National Film and Television Archive, Special Collection, London.)

4   Including 'the notorious' *Flaming Creatures* (1962) ('popular music as background to stylized images of masturbation, cross dressing, seduction

157

and rape'), *Christmas on Earth* (1963) (two reels of film projected on top of one another with reel A showing at full size and 'displaying close-ups of heterosexuality: penises, anuses, mouths and vaginas', while reel B was projected at half size (over reel A) and represented '1960s tabooed sex: interracial and homosexual') and *Scorpio Rising* (1963) (that combined 'homosexuality, popular culture, and camp satire' through the 'appropriation of images of male buddies from Hollywood movies, television and comics') (Staiger 2000: 139).

5 Kristin Thompson and David Bordwell trace the birth of the contemporary independent production company back to the early 1950s where companies such as Allied Artists and American International Pictures (AIP) were making quickly produced ('shot in a week or two') exploitation pictures that catered for the newly identified adolescent market. These films, including titles such as *I Was a Teenage Frankenstein* (1957); *Hot Rod Girl* (1956); *It Conquered the World* (1956) and *Shake Rattle and Roll* (1956) commercially 'exploited' the 'high schooler's' taste for horror, science fiction, juvenile crime and rock 'n' roll (Thompson and Bordwell 2003: 530).

6 In Hoberman's account the Whitney's Biennial showcase had become 'the preeminent institutional force in American avant-garde film [...] The biennial selection, which [was] subsequently packaged as a travelling show by the American Federation of Arts, [was] the most circulated exhibition of American a-g [avant-garde] film' (Hoberman 1991: 175–77).

7 Hoberman cites *Easy Rider* (1969), *American Graffiti* (1973) and *Mean Streets* (1973) in this context (1991: 175–76).

8 Copies of *The Elephant Man* UK lobby poster and *The Elephant Man* UK press book are held at the National Film and Television Archive, Special Collections, London.

9 Lynch goes further by suggesting that the 'tremendous sense of freedom' he enjoyed coincided with DEG's market flotation, since it was 'the littlest film [and] therefore the one that they [the accountants] didn't have to pay attention to' (Rodley 1997: 136).

10 The promotional trailer I have referred to is featured on the UK video release for *Peggy Sue Got Married* (CBS/Fox, no. 3800–50, 1987).

11 Charles Drazin has made the point that despite being 'the most talked about film of the eighties', in economic terms, *Blue Velvet* 'did good, but unexceptional business'. Made for $5m, as of February 1997 the film had returned $8,551,228 in US box office receipts (although this figure excludes domestic revenues). Thirty-five million US viewers tuned in to the pilot episode for *Twin Peaks* in April 1990 (Drazin 1998: 157).

Chapter 3

1 In his essay 'Realism and cinema: notes on some Brechtian theses', MacCabe likened George Elliot's novel *Middlemarch* to *Klute* (1971). MacCabe proposed that the narrative prose in both cases functions as a metalanguage that acts as a transparent 'voice of truth' that presides over, comments on and interprets the hierarchy of object languages (those articulated in the fictitious world of the narrative) that compose the classical realist novel and film. In *Middlemarch*, Elliot's descriptive authorial voice constitutes the metalanguage that allows 'reality to appear by denying its own status as articulation' while in cinema the 'voice of truth' is carried over to the camera (MacCabe 1974).

2 Despite rumours to the contrary within the *Dune* community, there are only two versions of the film: the original theatrical release timed at 135mins 56secs; and the television version timed at 180mins. Sean Murphy offers detailed comparisons of the two versions in relation to Lynch's original screenplay (seventh draft) in two articles: 'Building the perfect Dune, part one' (1986a) and 'Building the perfect Dune, part two' (1986b).

3 The Directors Guild of America introduced the pseudonym Allen Smithee in 1969 with the release of *Death of a Gunfighter*. Don Siegel replaced the film's original director, Robert Totten, during production with the upshot that neither wished to be credited as director. Jeremy Braddock and Stephen Hock suggest that Allen Smithee then 'became the pseudonym set aside by the Directors Guild of America for those directors who feel – or more importantly, can prove to the Guild's satisfaction – that their films have been taken out of their control'. They make no reference to Judas Booth although it seems quite reasonable to assume it served a similar function here with regard to screenwriting credits (Braddock and Hock 2001: 9).

4 *Dune Messiah* (1969), *Children of Dune* (1976), *God Emperor of Dune* (1981), *Heretics of Dune* (1984) and *Chapterhouse Dune* (1985).

5 There were five films in this cycle produced between 1967 and 1973: *Planet of the Apes* (1967), *Beneath the Planet of the Apes* (1970), *Escape from the Planet of the Apes* (1971), *Conquest of the Planet of the Apes* (1972) and *Battle for the Planet of the Apes* (1973). APJAC also produced a one-season 14-part television series for CBS that was broadcast in the US in 1974.

6 A videotaped copy of the interview between Auty, Lynch and De Laurentiis is held at the National Film and Television Archive in London. It is catalogued under David Lynch/*Dune* as 'The Guardian critic lecture', National Film Theatre, 23 January 1985.

7 Taken from the above interview.

8 I am indebted to the website Dune Index at www.arrakis.co.uk (accessed 10 May 2002) as a resource for this material. This site carries a comprehensive visual collection of *Dune* merchandise and memorabilia including a variety of *Dune's* international promotional posters and lobby cards, a *Dune* Collectors Survival Guide and pages displaying an array of *Dune* action figures and other tie-in merchandise.

9 The Dune Index at www.arrakis.co.uk, displays promotional posters from Germany (x4), France, America (x4), Spain (x2), Argentina, Mexico and a range of UK lobby promotional material. These include the original promotional poster, an eight-card British lobby card set featuring stills from the film 'The *Dune* movie promo poster card' and a *Dune* cinema leaflet.

10 The National Film and Television Archive in London holds hard copies of the UK poster and lobby cards, and a *Dune* press book. These materials are also displayed at the Dune Index at www.arrakis.co.uk.

11 The trailer I have referred to is featured as an extra on the widescreen video (theatrical) version of *Dune* (Universal, no. 0782463, 2000).

Chapter 4

1 We know this to be true of Lynch, who said of his itinerant upbringing 'I could feel what needed to be done to get along […] but it's really hard if you're on the outside, it forces you to want to get on the inside […] I had lots of friends but I loved being alone and looking at insects swarming in the garden […] there's happiness in one yard, one fence, or one piece of light on something. And hours could be spent in one tiny locale at the corner of the yard' (Rodley 1997: 3–13).

Chapter 5

1 This advertisement is reprinted in Collins (1993: 343).

2 As featured on the videocassette sleeve for *Twin Peaks,* programmes 1, 2 and 3, released through Screen Entertainments Ltd (no. SE 9141 1991).

3 Taken from the US promotional poster for *Wild at Heart* as featured in *The New York Times,* 19 August 1990, p.24.

4 Engels had been a co-writer on ten – 4, 10, 11, 13, 16, 19, 22, 25, 27 and 29 – of the series' 29 episodes.

Chapter 6

1   *Dumbland* is a series of eight three-minute computer animated films (drawn with a mouse) originally broadcast on Lynch's own website, while *The Angriest Dog in the World* was a weekly four-panel comic strip that appeared in the *LA Reader* between 1983 and 1992.

2   *American Chronicles* was produced in 1991 through the Lynch/Frost production company. Lynch acted (with Frost) as Executive Producer and as Co-director for a single contribution.

3   Lynch directed the first of a series of fragrance commercials as early as 1988 for Calvin Klein's 'Obsession' (this was a series of four commercials romantically themed on the works of famous literary authors such as F. Scott Fitzgerald and D.H. Lawrence) and followed with 'Gio' ('Who is Gio?') and 'Opium' commercials for Giorgio Armani and Yves Saint Laurent respectively in 1992. Later Lynch worked on 'Tresor' for Lancôme Paris and 'The Instinct for Life' for Jill Sander's 'Background' fragrance in 1993. In 1994 he directed a commercial for the 'Sun Moon Stars' fragrance for Karl Lagerfield and, in 2008, a commercial 'Gucci by Gucci' for Gucci. Lynch has also directed advertisements for 'Alka-Seltzer Plus' and 'Barilla Pasta' in 1993, and a set of three commercials for the 'Clear Blue Easy' pregnancy test in 1997. Additionally Lynch made two televised public service shorts 'We Care about New York', which addressed the city's rat infestation, in 1991 and in 1993 'Revealed', a film commissioned by the American Cancer Society promoting breast cancer awareness.

4   The narrow range of literature that does address Lynch's commercial work tends to justify his wealth not in terms of 'selling out' but for the artistic opportunities it opens up. On a rare occasion when Lynch was drawn on this issue, he spoke of the 'freeing power of money' as being 'a very healing sort of thing' since (as artists) 'all we want to do … is to be able to do what we want [to] get the sense of freedom' (Breskin 1990).

5   The Japanese held a special fondness for *Twin Peaks*. In an article written in 1992, Terry McCarthy reported on a number of other commercial initiatives that included a *Twin Peaks* package tour (organised by the Japanese Tourist Bureau) and Japan's very own imitation *Twin Peaks*, on the Island Maetsue, and for which Japanese railways advertised routes to the island through posters showing mountains and a sign 'Welcome to Twin Peaks'. Indeed, McCarthy reported that 'David Lynch's taste for the bizarre and the macabre' had struck a cord with the Japanese and that earlier that year 'Twin Peaks fans set an altar in memory of Laura Palmer in Shinjuku station, the busiest station in Japan (and the world). Pictures of Laura and a dummy model wrapped in plastic were

adorned with wreaths by mourning fans – a ray of spirituality in the morning rush hour' (McCarthy 1992).

6 These and the majority of Lynch's other commercials and promos were viewed at 'David Lynch, Commercials, Ads and Promos' at www.lynchnet.com/ads/ (accessed 12 November 2003). Most of these may also be found through the YouTube website.

7 The website www.lynchnet.com/ads/ records this campaign. Lynch's commercial was viewed at www.idmproductions.fr/main/index (accessed 25 August 2004) and is also available for viewing on YouTube titled 'David Lynch's wacky cigarette ad'.

8 'The third place', 'Bambi' and 'Rabbits' can all be viewed at YouTube.

9 Original article reproduced in 'carpages.co.uk', reprinted at, www.lynchnet.com/ads/, accessed 11 November 2003.

10 Lynch's film was the third in a series of '"Lady Dior" noir mini-features' that had started in 'May 2009 with *Lady Noire*, directed by Olivier Dahan (*La Vie en Rose*). Part two appeared in January [2010]: *Lady Rouge*, directed by music video and film director Jonas Akerlund'. The film can be viewed at www.ladydior.com (Copping 2010 (reprinted at www.FT.com/cms), accessed 22 May 2010).

Chapter 7

1 As described by the film's production company, StudioCanal, on its website www.studiocanal.com/movie/mulhollanddrive, accessed 7 February 2004.

2 The network for whom Lynch had worked previously on both *Twin Peaks* and *On the Air*.

3 This trailer was viewed at www.mulhollanddrive.com, accessed, 14 October 2003.

4 For instance, www.mulhollanddrive.com carried 'Bios', 'Chat' (a transcript of an interview with Lynch), 'Stills' (of Lynch and stars at Cannes Film Festival) and so on, and the *Mulholland Dr.* DVD (released through Universal in the UK in 2002, catalogue no. 9031299) which features as 'Extras' cast and crew biographies, interviews and so on.

5 A transcript of this interview can be found at: www.geocities.com/Hollywood/2093/lynch.html, accessed 16 December 2003.

Bibliography

Allen, Robert C., 'From exhibition to reception: reflections on the audience in film history', in A. Kuhn and J. Stacey (eds), *Screen Histories, A Screen Reader* (Oxford, Clarendon Press, 1998)

Atkinson, Michael, *Blue Velvet BFI Modern Classics* (London, BFI, 1997)

Barthes, Roland, *The Pleasure of the Text* (Oxford, Blackwell, 1975a)

Barthes, Roland, *S/Z* (London, Jonathan Cape, 1975b)

Barthes, Roland, 'The death of the author', in J. Caughie (ed.), *Theories of Authorship* (London, Routledge, 1981)

Bazin, André, 'La politique des auteurs', in J. Caughie (ed.), *Theories of Authorship* (London, Routledge, 1981)

Benjamin, Walter, 'The work of art in the age of mechanical reproduction', in *Illuminations* (London, Fontana, 1973)

Bordwell, David, *Ozu and the Poetics of Cinema* (London, BFI, 1988)

Bordwell, David, 'The art cinema as a mode of film practice', in L. Braudy and M. Cohen (eds), *Film Theory and Criticism* (New York, Oxford University Press, 1999)

Braddock, Jeremy and Hock, Stephen, *Directed by Allen Smithee* (Minneapolis MN, University of Minnesota Press, 2001)

Bundtzen, Lynda K., '"Don't look at me": woman's body, woman's voice in *Blue Velvet*', *Western Humanities Review* 42/3 (1998)

Cameron, Ian, 'Films, directors and critics', in J. Caughie (ed.), *Theories of Authorship* (London, BFI, 1981)

Caughie, John (ed.), *Theories of Authorship* (London, BFI, 1981)

Chion, Michel, *David Lynch* (London, BFI, 1996)

Chisholm, Brad, 'Difficult viewing: the pleasure of complex screen narratives', *Critical Studies in Mass Communication* 8/4, December (1991)

Collins, Jim, 'Television and postmodernism', in R.C. Allen (ed.), *Channels of Discourse Reassembled* (University of North Carolina Press, 1993)

163

Corrigan, Timothy, *A Cinema Without Walls: Movies and Culture After Vietnam* (New York, Routledge, 1991)

Corrigan, Timothy, 'Auteurs and the new Hollywood', in J. Lewis (ed.), *The New American Cinema* (Durham NC and London, Duke University Press, 1998)

Creed, Barbara, 'A journey through *Blue Velvet*, film, fantasy and the female spectator', *New Formations* 6, Winter (1988)

Drazin, Charles, *On Blue Velvet* (London, Bloomsbury, 1998)

Duchamp, Marcel, 'The creative act', in M. Sanovillet and E. Peterson (eds), *The Essential Writings of Marcel Duchamp* (London, Thames and Hudson, 1975)

Elsaesser, Thomas, 'Specularity and engulfment, Francis Ford Coppola and Bram Stoker's Dracula', in S. Neale and M. Smith (eds), *Contemporary Hollywood Cinema* (London, Routledge, 1998)

Foucault, Michel, 'What is an author?', in J. Caughie (ed.), *Theories of Authorship* (London, BFI, 1981)

Freud, Sigmund, *Totem and Taboo* (New York, W.W. Norton, 1950)

Freud, Sigmund, 'Beyond the pleasure principle', in P. Gay (ed.), *The Freud Reader* (London, Vintage, 1989)

Freud, Sigmund, *Introductory Lectures on Psychoanalysis* (London, Penguin, 1991)

Friend, Tad, 'Creative differences', *New Yorker* 30 August and 6 September 1999 (reprinted as a whole at *www.lynchnet.com/mulhollanddrive*, accessed 21 November 2003)

Frost, Mark, *The Autobiography of F.B.I. Special Agent Dale Cooper: My Life, My Tapes* (New York, Pocket Books, 1991)

Frost, Mark and Saul Wurman, Richard, *Welcome to Twin Peaks: An Access Guide to the Town* (New York, Pocket Books, 1991)

Fuchs, Cynthia J., '"I looked for you in my closet tonight", voyeurisms and victims in *Blue Velvet*', *Journey of Archetype and Culture* 49, Spring (1989)

Gaut, Berys, 'Film authorship and collaboration', in R. Allen and M. Smith (eds), *Film Theory and Philosophy* (Oxford, Oxford University Press, 1997)

Gerstner, A. David and Staiger, J. (eds), *Authorship and Film* (New York, AFI, 2003)

Gunning, Tom, 'The cinema of attractions: early film, its spectator and the avant-garde', *Wide Angle* 8 2/4 (1986)

Herbert, Frank, 'The origins of Dune', in T. O'Reilly (ed.), *Frank Herbert, The Maker of Dune, Insights of a Master of Science Fiction* (New York, Berkeley CA, 1987)

Herbert, Frank, *Dune* (London, Corgi Books, 1998)

Hoberman, J., *Vulgar Modernism, Writings on Movies and Other Media* (Philadelphia PA, Temple University Press, 1991)

Hoberman, J. and Rosenbaum, Jonathan, *Midnight Movies* (New York, Harper and Row, 1983)

Holub, Robert C., *Reception Theory, A Critical Introduction* (London, Methuen, 1984)

Hughes, David, *The Complete Lynch* (London, Virgin, 2002)

Iser, Wolfgang, *The Act of Reading, A Theory of Aesthetic Response* (London, Routledge & Kegan Paul, 1978)

Jameson, Fredric, 'Nostalgia for the present', *The South Atlantic Quarterly* 88/2 (1989)

Jameson, Fredric, 'The deconstruction of expression' in C. Harrison and P. Wood (eds), *Art in Theory 1900–1990* (Cambridge, Blackwell, 1994)

Jauss, Hans Robert, *Toward an Aesthetic of Reception* (The Harvester Press, University of Minnesota, 1982)

Jenkins, Henry, *Textual Poachers, Television Fans and Participatory Culture* (New York, Routledge, 1992)

Kaleta, Kenneth C., *David Lynch* (New York, Twayne Publishing, 1995)

Klinger, Barbara, *Melodrama and Meaning, History, Culture, and the Films of Douglas Sirk* (Bloomington IN, Indiana University Press, 1994)

Lavery, David (ed.), *Full of Secrets: Critical Approaches to Twin Peaks* (Wayne State University Press, 1994)

Lavery, David (ed.), 'Peaked out!', *Film/Literature Quarterly* 24/4 (1993)

Layton, Lynne, 'Blue Velvet: a parable of male development', *Screen* 35/4, Winter (1994)

Le Blanc, Michelle, and Odell, Colin, *David Lynch, Pocket Essential Films* (Harpenden, Pocket Essentials, 2000)

Lenz, Joseph M., 'Manifest destiny: science fiction and classical form', in G.E. Slusser, E.S. Rabkin and R. Scholes (eds), *Coordinates, Placing Science Fiction and Fantasy* (Carbondale IL, Southern Illinois University Press, 1983)

Livingston, Paisley, 'Cinematic authorship', in R. Allen and M. Smith (eds), *Film Theory and Philosophy* (Oxford, Oxford University Press, 1997)

Lynch, David, *Catching the Big Fish: Meditation, Consciousness, and Creativity* (London, Penguin, 2006)

Lynch, Jennifer, *The Secret Diary of Laura Palmer* (New York, Pocket Books, 1990)

MacCabe, Colin, 'Realism and cinema: notes on some Brechtian theses', *Screen* 15/2, Summer (1974)

Mactaggart, Allister, *The Film Paintings of David Lynch, Challenging Film Theory* (Bristol, Intellect Ltd, 2010)

Medhurst, Andy, 'That special thrill: Brief Encounter, homosexuality and authorship', *Screen* 32/2, Summer (1991)

Mercer, Kobena, 'Skin head sex thing, radical difference and the homoerotic imaginary', in Bad Object Choices (eds), *How Do I look? Queer Film and Video* (Seattle WA, Bay Press, 1991)

Mulvey, Laura, 'Netherworlds and the unconscious: Oedipus and *Blue Velvet*', *Fetishism and Curiosity* (London, BFI, 1996)

Mulvey, Laura, 'Visual pleasure and narrative cinema', in L. Braudy and M. Cohen (eds), *Film Theory and Criticism 5th edition* (Oxford, Oxford University Press, 1999)

Nana, Ed, *The Making of Dune* (Berkeley CA, MCA Publishing, 1985)

Neale, Steve, 'New Hollywood cinema', *Screen* 17/2, Summer (1976)

Nochimson, Martha P., *The Passion of David Lynch, Wild at Heart in Hollywood* (Austin TX, University of Texas Press, 1997)

Olson, Greg, *David Lynch, Beautiful Dark* (Lanham MD, Scarecrow Press, 2008)

Orvell, Miles, *The Real Thing, Imitation and Authenticity in American Culture 1880–1940* (London, Chapel Hill NC, 1989)

Quart, Leonard and Auster, Albert, *American Film and Society since 1945* (London, Macmillan, 1984)

Ramsay, Christine, 'Twin Peaks, mountains or molehills?', *Cineaction* 24/5, August (1991)

Roberts, Adam, *Science Fiction, the New Critical Idiom* (London and New York, Routledge, 2000)

Rodley, Chris, *Lynch on Lynch* (London, Faber and Faber, 1997)

Sarris, Andrew, 'Towards a theory of film history', in J. Caughie (ed.), *Theories of Authorship* (London, BFI, 1981)

Shattuc, Jane M. 'Postmodern misogyny in *Blue Velvet*', *Genders* 13, Spring (1992)

Staiger, Janet, *Interpreting Films, Studies in the Historical Reception of American Cinema* (Princeton NJ, Princeton University Press, 1992)

Staiger, Janet, *Perverse Spectators, the Practices of Film Reception* (New York, New York University Press, 2000)

Staiger, Janet, 'Authorship approaches', in D.A. Gerstner and J. Staiger (eds), *Authorship and Film* (New York, AFI, 2003)

Stern, Lesley, 'The oblivious transfer: analysing *Blue Velvet*', *Camera Obscura* 30: May (1993)

Sutherland, J.A., 'American science fiction since 1960', in P. Parrinder (ed.), *Science Fiction, A Critical Guide* (London, Longman, 1979)

Thompson, Kirsten and Bordwell, David, *Film History, an Introduction, International Edition* (Boston MA, McGraw-Hill, 2003)

Tomashevskii, Boris, 'Literature and biography', in L. Matejka and K. Pomorska (eds), *Readings in Russian Poetics* (Cambridge MA, MIT Press, 1971)

Tudor, Andrew, *Theories of Film* (London, Secker and Warburg/BFI, 1974)

Williamson, Judith, *Consuming Passions* (London, Marion Boyars, 1987)

Wolfe, Gary K., 'Autoplastic and alloplastic adaptations in science fiction: "waldo" and "desertion"', in G.E. Slusser, E.S. Rabkin and R. Scholes (eds), *Coordinates, Placing Science Fiction and Fantasy* (Carbondale IL, Southern Illinois Press, 1983)

Wollen, Peter, 'The auteur theory, michael curtiz, and *casablanca*' (sic), in D.A. Gerstner and J. Staiger (eds), *Authorship and Film* (New York, Routledge, 2003)

Woods, David A., *Weirdsville USA, The Obsessive Universe of David Lynch* (London, Plexus, 2000)

Wyatt, Justin, *High Concepts, Movies and Marketing in Hollywood* (Austin TX, University of Texas Press, 1996)

Articles, Reviews and Publicity

Adair, Gilbert, 'The real thing', *The Listener,* 17 January 1985

Adair, Gilbert, 'Where the grass is always greener', *The Independent on Sunday*, 5 December 1999

Andrew, Geoff, 'Sex shocker or cult classic?', *Time Out*, 4–11 March 1987

Andrew, Geoff, 'Start making sense', *Time Out*, 20 August 1997

Andrew, Geoff, 'Twin Peaks: Fire Walk with Me', in J. Pym (ed.), *Time Out Film Guide* (London, Penguin Books, 2000)

Andrews, Nigel, 'Eraserhead', *Financial Times*, 30 December 1979

Andrews, Nigel, 'Twin Peaks: Fire Walk with Me', *Financial Times*, 19 November 1992

Baker, Henry, 'The Elephant Man', *Cineaste* XI (1981)

Bennet, Ray, 'Inland Empire', *The Hollywood Reporter*, 30 October 2006

Berry, Betsy, 'Forever, in my dreams: generic conventions and the subversive imagination in Blue Velvet', *Literature/Film Quarterly* XVI/2, April (1988)

Billson, Anne, 'A coup for the king of weirdness', *Sunday Correspondent*, 26 August 1990

Bremner, Charles, 'Surrealist soap hailed as a TV turning point', *The Times*, 12 April 1990

Breskin, David, 'I was sort of embarrassed that my parents were so normal', *Rolling Stone,* No. 586, 6 September (1990)

Brown, Geoff, 'Sharing can be bad for your health', *The Times*, 19 November 1992

Brown, Geoff, 'Lost Highway', *The Times*, 26 March 1998

Brown, Scott, 'Best schizo sweetie', *Entertainment Weekly*, 21–28 December 2001, reproduced at www.ew.com/ew/report/0,6115,252809_7|30578||0_00.html, accessed 10 March 2005

Calhoun, Dave, 'Inland Empire', *Time Out*, 17–13 March 2007: issue 1907, reprinted at www.timeout.com/film/reviews/84073/Inland_Empire.html (accessed 19 October 2009)

Cart, 'Dune', *Variety*, 5 December 1985

Cart, 'Blue Velvet', *Variety* CCCXXIV/6, 3 September 1986

Charity, Tom, 'Mulholland Drive', *Time Out*, 9 January 2002

Christy, Desmond, 'Peaks and pique', *The Guardian*, 4 September 1992

Combs, Richard, 'The Elephant Man', *Monthly Film Bulletin* XCVII/561, October (1980)

Combs, Richard, 'Crude thoughts and fierce forces', *Monthly Film Bulletin* LIV/639, April (1987)

Copping, Nicola, 'David Lynch's new film for Dior', *The Financial Times*, 14 May 2010 (reprinted at www.FT.com/cms), accessed 22 May 2010

Cousins, Mark, *David Lynch, Scene by Scene* (BBC television, first transmitted in the UK, 28 November 1999)

Cumbow, Robert C., 'Eraserhead', *Movietone News*, 14 August 1978

Cunningham, Tessa, 'Peak a twinning formula', *The Sun*, 27 February 1991

David, Anna, 'Twin piques', *Premiere*, November (2001)

Dargis, Manohla, 'Old masters', *Film Comment*, July/August (2001)

Day-Lewis, Sean, 'The peak of the season', *Broadcast*, 23 November 1990

Elley, Derek, 'The Elephant Man', *Films* 1/2, January (1981)

Eraserhead UK Press Book (1978) (copy held at the National Film and Television Archive, London)

'The forty most internationally important directors', reprinted at: Film.guardian.co.uk/features/page/0,11456,1082823.00.html 22.12.2003, accessed 24 February 2004

Francis, Pam, 'Who cares about Laura Palmer'?, *Today*, 12 December 1990

French, Sean, 'The heart of the cavern', *Sight and Sound*, Spring (1987)

Fuller, Graham, 'Babes in Babylon', *Sight and Sound*, December (2001)

Gallivan, John, 'State of shock', *The Independent*, 14 November 1991

Gilby, Ryan, 'Moments that made the year', *The Independent*, 26 December 1997

Godwin, George, K., 'Eraserhead', *Film Quarterly* XXXIX/1, Fall (1985)

Goldstein, Warren, 'Incest for the millions', *Commonweal*, December (1990)

Guider, 'Twin Peaks', *Variety*, 4 April 1990

Heal, Sue, 'Lynch's peak of perfection', *Today*, 27 October 1990

Heal, Sue, 'Twin Peaks: Fire Walk with Me', *Today*, 20 November 1992

Heyn, Christopher, 'The Straight Story', *Christian Spotlight on the Movies* (1999), reproduced at www.christiananswers.net/spotlight/reviews/thestraightstory.html (accessed 10 March 2000)

Higgins, Mike, 'Lost Highway', *The Independent*, 13 March 1998

Hoberman, J., 'Review of Eraserhead and Angel City', *The Village Voice*, 24 October 1977

Ind, Nicholas, 'Adidas earn their stripes', *The Guardian*, 16 August 1993

'Inland Empire keywords', http://www.imdb.com/title/tt0460829/keywords, accessed 3 February 2010

Jacobs, A.J., 'David Lynch takes a pregnancy pause', *Entertainment Weekly*, 18 July 1997

Jenkins, Steve, 'Blue Velvet', *Monthly Film Bulletin* LIV/639, April (1987)

Johnson, Sheila, 'Twin Peaks', *The Independent*, 12 December 1989

Johnstone, Iain, 'Twin Peaks: Fire Walk with Me', *Sunday Times*, 22 November 1992, Section 8

Kael, Pauline, 'The current cinema, out there and in here', *The New Yorker*, 22 September 1986

Kenny, Glenn, 'Mulholland Drive review', *Premiere*, October (2001), reproduced at www.mulhollanddrive.com/press.html, accessed 19 March 2005

King, Clive, 'Going Straight', *The Times*, 5 September 1998

Lane, Anthony, 'The dirt road to Lustville USA', *The Independent on Sunday*, 26 August 1990

Lawson, Mark, 'Red herrings and cherry pie', *The Independent on Sunday*, 28 October 1990

L'Ecuyer, Gerard, 'David Lynch, out of bounds', *Interview* 17/3 (1987)

Lim, Dennis, 'Return of the Lynch mob', *The Independent on Sunday*, 23 February 1997

Lynch, David, *Dune*, 'The Guardian critic lecture', National Film Theatre, 23 January 1985

Lynch, David, *Made in America Interviews*, 1993 (recording held at the National Film and Television Archive, Special Collection, London)

Lynch, Jennifer, 'The secret diary of Lara Palmer', serialisation in *The Mail on Sunday*, 1990

Lyons, Donald, 'La-la limbo', *Film Comment*, January/February (1997)

Lyttle, John, 'When the Log Lady sings', *The Independent*, 18 June 1991

Mack, 'Eraserhead', *Variety*, 23 March 1977

Mandell, Paul, 'Photography and visual effects in Dune', *American Cinematographer*, December 1984

Mantel, Hilary, 'Don't take the vicar', *Spectator*, 1 September 1990, reproduced at www.davidlynch.de/wildspec.html, accessed 27 May 2001

Mather, Victoria, 'Welcome weirdos', *Evening Standard*, 24 October 1990

McCarthy, Terry, 'Out of Japan', *The Independent*, 17 August 1992

McCarthy, Todd, 'Twin Peaks: Fire Walk with Me', *Variety*, 18 May 1992

McCarthy, Todd, 'Lost Highway', *Variety*, 20 January 1997

McGuigan, Cathleen, 'Black and blue is beautiful', *Newsweek*, 27 October 1986

Middlehurst, Lester, 'The wacky soap you have to quote to prove you are not a philistine', *Today*, 5 May 1990

Morley, Sheridan, 'Twin Peaks: Fire Walk with Me', *The Sunday Express*, 22 November 1992

Muir, Kate, 'No more Mr. nice guy', *The Times*, 30 August 1997

Murphy, Sean, 'Building the perfect Dune, part one', *Video Watchdog* 33 (1986a)

Murphy, Sean, 'Building the perfect Dune, part two', *Video Watchdog* 34 (1986b)

Murray, Scott, 'Twin Peaks: Fire Walk with Me, the press conference', *Cinema Papers* No. 89 August, 1992

Nadelson, Reggie, 'A nation gripped by something very weird', *The Independent*, 23 May 1990

Paterson, Peter, 'Peak show goes over the top', *Daily Mail*, 7 November 1990

Pearson, Harry, 'Twin Peaks: Fire Walk with Me', *Films in Review* XLIII, 1992

Penman, Ian, 'Smalltown America under the microscope', *Sunday Correspondent*, 9 July 1990

Pourroy, Janine, and Shay, Don, 'The shape of Dune', *Cinefex* 21, April (1985)

Purgavie, Dermot, 'Are you ready for Twin Peaks?', *The Mail on Sunday*, 4 August 1990

Pym, John, 'I pray to god he is an idiot, The Elephant Man', *Sight and Sound*, 50 Winter (1980/81)

Quinn, Anthony, 'It's great to be straight', *The Independent*, 3 December 1999

Rafferty, Terrence, 'The current cinema: one thing after another', *The New Yorker*, 9 April 1990a

Rafferty, Terrence, 'End of the road', *The New Yorker*, 27 August 1990b

Rodley, Chris, 'Strange. The man seems so normal', *The Independent*, 26 November 1999

Romney, Jonathan, 'Mr. Weird plays it straight', *The Guardian*, November 1999, reproduced at www.davidlynch.de/99guardian.html (accessed 24 June 2000)

Russell, John, 'Time to get clued up on Peakspeak', *The Sunday Express*, 28 October 1990

'Ruth, roses and revolvers: David Lynch presents the surrealists', *Arena Special* (BBC Television, first transmitted in the UK 10 April 1987)

Sarris, Andrew, 'The American cinema', *Film Culture* (1963)

Sharrett, Christopher, 'Wild at Heart', *Cineaste* XVIII/2 (1991)

Simon, John, 'Neat trick', *National Review*, 7 November 1986

Sloman, Tony, 'Dune', *Films and Filming* 364, January (1985)

Stoddard, Patrick, 'Topping off those peaks', *The Times*, 16 December 1990

Taylor, Paul, 'Eraserhead', *Monthly Film Bulletin*, March (1979)

The Elephant Man UK Press Book (1980) (held at the National Film and Television Archive, Special Collections, London)

Thompson, David, 'Hollywood's hitman: Quentin Tarantino', *The Independent on Sunday*, 23 October 1994

Turan, Kenneth, 'Farnsworth earnestness cuts through Lynch's "story"', *LA Times Calendar*, 15 October 1999, reproduced at www.davidlynch.de/latss.html (accessed 31 May 2000)

'Twin Peaks', *The Independent*, 3 February 1991

'The Twin Peaks Press Kit': reprinted at www.twinpeaks.org/archives/press, accessed 17 May 2004

Walker, Alexander, 'Artificial heart', *Evening Standard*, 23 August 1990

Walker, Alexander, 'Twin Peaks: Fire Walk with Me', *Evening Standard*, 19 November 1992

Walters, Margaret, 'Queasy rider', *The Listener*, 23 August 1990

www.dallas.tvtome.com, accessed 17 May 2004

Weissberg, Jay, 'Inland Empire', *Variety*, 6 September 2006

'Wild at Heart print advertisement', *The New York Times*, 19 August 1990

Zoglin, Richard, 'A sleeper with a dream', *Time Magazine (US Edition)*, 21 May 1990

Selected Web Sources

www.arrakis.co.uk

www.geocities.com/Hollywood/2093/lynch.html

www.idmproductions.fr/main/index

www.ladydior.com

www.lynchnet.com/ads/

www.mulhollanddrive.com/press.html

www.studiocanal.com/movie/mulhollanddrive

www.twinpeaks.org/archives/press

www.YouTube.com

Index

2001: A Space Odyssey (novel)
(1968) 44

ABC (television network)
136–41
Advise and Consent (1962) 3
Almodóvar, Pedro 23
Alphabet, The (1968) 16, 106, 157
Altman, Robert 4
American Chronicles (television
documentary series) (1990)
111, 161
American Express credit cards
(advertisement) 113, 115
American Film Institute (AFI)
16–17, 113
American Film Institute, Centre for
Advanced Film Studies 17
American Graffiti (1973) 158
American Underground Cinema
('New American Cinema
Group') 19–22, 158
American Werewolf in London, An
(1981) 112
Amputee, The (1974) 106

Analog (science-fiction magazine)
44
Angriest Dog in the World, The (*LA
Reader* 1983–92) 161
Armani, Giorgio 113
Atkinson, Michael 29, 43, 58–59
auteurism/auteurist/theories of
authorship 1–6, 8–13, 14–15,
18–19, 32, 35, 37–44, 51, 54,
56–57, 59–63, 64–67, 69, 70,
72, 73, 75–76, 83, 86–90, 92,
96, 98, 101, 106, 108, 112,
118, 120–28, 131–36, 141,
148, 154, 156
early auteurism 3, 43, 64–65, 148,
155
la politique des auteurs (Bazin) 57,
92, 128, 152
television auteurism 88–92, 96,
100
'author function' (Foucault) 40
*Autobiography of FBI Special Agent
Dale Cooper, My Life, My
Times, The* (series tie-in
book) (1991) 97

Auty, Chris 50, 159

avant-garde cinema 15, 19, 21–23, 70, 76, 100, 102, 108–9, 155, 158

Bad (Michael Jackson) (1987) 112

Badalamenti, Angelo 37, 123

Bancroft, Anne 26

Barenholtz, Ben 17

Barthes, Roland 5–6, 10, 38–41, 43–44, 60–63, 64–65, 67, 80, 83, 124, 135, 148, 152

Bazin, André 18, 92, 122, 135, 152–53

Bells are Ringing, The (1960) 128

Benjamin, Walter 153

Bergen, Eric 48

Berry, Betsy 31

Best Man, The (1964) 3

Bilal, Enki 117

'biographical legend' (concept of) 8, 14

Black or White (Michael Jackson) (1991) 112

Blow Job (1964) 22

Blue Velvet (1986) 1, 7, 14, 16, 23, 38

  box-office returns 158

  critical theory/Lynch as author of 64–67, 69, 72, 83

  feminist reception of 65–78

  Freudian themes in 69, 71, 73–74, 86, 93, 101, 104, 110, 133, 146, 150

  Jeffrey Beaumont/MacLachlan as Lynch's alter ego 58–60

  lack of realism and inner truth in Jameson's criticism of 68–71

  Lynch's position in marketing of 28–36

Bordwell, David 8, 64, 100

Breton, André 35

Broadcast Magazine 97

Brooks, Mel 18

Bundtzen, Lynda K. 74

Cage, Nicolas 102

Cahiers du Cinéma/Cahiers Group 3, 11, 54, 122, 143, 152

Camera One (French production company) 47

Cameron, Ian 127, 128

Cannes Film Festival 102, 104

Casablanca (1942) 128

Catching the Big Fish, Meditation, Consciousness, and Creativity (2006) 129

Caughie, John 3, 127

Cawston, Tim 33

Chaplin, Charlie 7

Chelsea Girls, The (1966) 22

Chion, Michel 43, 59, 60, 106, 109–11

Chisholm, Brad 88–89, 94

Chodorow, Nancy 77

Christian Dior 120–21

Christian Spotlight at the Movies 127

Christmas on Earth (1963) 158

CIBY-2000 104

cinéma pur 100

cine-structuralism 133

ciné-vérité 100

'Clear Blue Easy' pregnancy test advertisement 117

Colbys, The (1985–87) 94

Collins, Jim 95–96

Coppola, Francis Ford 4

Cornfeld, Stuart 18, 26

Corrigan, Timothy 2, 32, 35

Cotillard, Marion 120–21

'Cowboy and the Frenchman, The'
  (1988) 106

Creed, Barbara 75

crime thriller 4

critical theory 64–67, 69, 72, 75, 83

Curtiz, Michael 122–23, 127–28,
  140–41

Dada 4

Dallas (1978–91) 93–95

Dangerous (Michael Jackson) (1991)
  112

'Death of the Author, The' (Barthes) 5,
  10, 38–40, 43, 155

Death of a Gunfighter (1969) 159

DEG (De Laurentiis Entertainment
  Group) 28, 29, 158

De Laurentiis, Dino 28, 29, 48, 49,
  54

De Laurentiis, Rafaella 28, 48, 49
  on hiring Lynch as director of Dune
  50–51

de Man, Paul 11, 12, 64

De Palma, Brian 4

Deren, Maya 21

Dern, Laura 102, 123, 129

de Vore, Christopher 48

Directors Guild of America 159

Disney, Buena Vista International 138

Drazin, Charles 57

Dreams that Money Can Buy (1947)
  34–35

Duchamp, Marcel x, 35

Dumbland (2002) 161

Dune (1984) 14–15, 18, 28–29, 37–38,
  101, 110, 159
  compound authorships in 41–56
  as a Lynch film 56–63
  'Special TV Edition' 44
Dune novels/symbolism in
  44–47
  Dune Messiah (1969), Children of
    Dune (1976), God Emperor of
    Dune (1981), Heretics of Dune
    (1984), Chapterhouse Dune
    (1985) 159
Dynasty (1981–89) 94

Easy Rider (1969) 158

Elephant Man, The (1980) 14, 18,
  25–28, 33, 43, 48, 51, 110

Elmes, Frederick 37

Elsaesser, Thomas 4

El Topo (1971) 17, 25

Emak-Bakia (1926) 34

Engels, Robert 104

Entertainment Weekly 117, 150

Eraserhead (1976) 1, 14, 33, 35, 51,
  110
  legacy to the avant-garde 17–21
  as midnight movie 23–28

Ernst, Max 34–35

Excalibur (1981) 53

Expressionism 4

Farnsworth, Richard 126

Ferrara, Abel 4

Financial Times 120

Flaming Creatures (1962) 158

Formalism 4, 9

  Russian formalism 8

  Soviet formalism 100

Foucault, Michel 15, 40, 41, 43, 44, 148

fragrance commercials 161

Francis, Freddie 26, 28, 123

  on low key colour for *Dune* 50

French structuralism 8

Freud, Sigmund 61, 63, 66–67, 73, 76, 78

  attributes of the artist/the 'pleasure principle' 79–84, 129

Friend, Tad ('Creative Differences') 136–40

Friends (1994–2004) 137

Frost, Mark 90

Fuchs, Cynthia 65, 72, 74

Galliano, John 120

Garbutt, Chris 118

Gaut, Berys 42

Georgia Coffee commercials (1993) 116

Gerstner, David A. 2

Gifford, Barry 102, 123–24

Godard, Jean-Luc 117

Godwin, K. George 25

Grandmother, The (1970) 16, 106

Grazer, Brian 139

Griffith, D. W. 5

Guardian 2003 league table of the 40 most internationally important working directors 154

Gucci 113

Harring, Laura Elena 143, 144, 150

Hawks, Howard 122

Herbert, Frank

  as author of *Dune* 38, 41–44, 48, 49, 56, 57

  endorsement of *Dune* movie 54

  worldview in *Dune* novel 45–47

Hitchcock, Alfred 5, 122

  Alfred Hitchcock Presents 89

Hoberman, J. 14, 15, 22, 23, 24, 26, 31, 43, 62, 158

Hollywood Reporter, The 131

Holub, Robert C. 11

Hopkins, Anthony 26

Hopper, Dennis 31

'horizons of expectation'/horizontal paradigms 5, 7–13, 31, 35, 39, 44, 56, 58, 62, 89–90, 92, 95, 98, 100–1, 104, 107, 108, 120, 125, 134, 137, 138, 143, 144–46, 148, 149, 152

horror films 4

Hot Rod Girl (1956) 158

Hughes, David 106, 109

Hurt, John 26

Imagine Television 139

Industrial Symphony No. 1: The Dream of the Broken Hearted (1991) 110

INLAND EMPIRE (2006) 38, 101, 108,
    111, 121, 123, 124, 134
and transcendental meditation
    129–32
Iser, Wolfgang 5, 7, 9
I Was a Teenage Frankenstein (1957)
    158
It Conquered the World (1956) 158

Jacobs, Arthur P. (APJAC production
    company) 47
Jameson, Fredric 65, 67, 70, 71, 76
Jauss, Hans Robert (see also 'horizons
    of expectation') 5, 7, 9–13, 89,
    96, 100–1
Jenkins, Henry 12, 87–88
Jodorowsky, Alejandro 17, 48

Kael, Pauline 35, 66
Kaleta, Kenneth 109
Kapsis, Robert 7
Kiss (1963) 22
Klein, Calvin 113
Klinger, Barbara 2, 7, 8
Klute (1971) 159
Kramer, Stanley 28
Krantz, Tony 137, 140
Kusturica, Emir 117

Lady Blue Shanghai (2010) 120–21,
    162
Landis, John 112
Late Night with David Letterman
    96
Lavery, David 87

Layton, Lynne 73, 76–78
Le Blanc, Michelle and Colin Odell
    57
Lee, Sheryl 92
Leno, Jay 149–50
Lenz, Joseph M. 45
Livingston, Paisley 12, 41, 42, 83
Lost Highway (1997) 101, 108, 110, 111,
    123–26, 132, 137
Lucas, George 4, 49
Lumière and Company (1995) 106
Lynch, David
  childhood/family upbringing
    78–79
  as 'Eagle Scout' 157
  legacy of the movie brats 1, 4
  likeness to Frank Capra and Jimmy
    Stewart 35, 66
  love for the French 131
  MacLachlan as Lynch alter ego 35,
    58–59
  on commercials 113
  on relationship with industry 157
  on wealth 161

MacCabe, Colin, 39, 159
MacLachlan, Kyle 31, 37
  as Agent Cooper 58, 92–93
  as Jeffrey Beaumont/Lynch's alter ego
    35, 58–59
  as Paul Atreides 57–59
Magritte, René 118
Manchurian Candidate, The (1962) 3
Man Ray 34
Marxism 65, 69, 83, 110

Masland, Charles 7

Masters, Anthony 52, 62

Mayersberg, Paul 127

Mean Streets (1973) 158

Medhurst, Andy 67, 134

Mekas, Jonas 21, 25

Mellancamp, Patricia (summary of
    'The First Statement of the New
    American Cinema Group') 19

melodrama 4

Mercer, Kobena 67, 134

Middlemarch (novel) (1871–72) 159

midnight movies 17–18, 22–25

Minnelli, Vincente 128

modernism 69–70, 155

modernist criticism 106, 110, 120

Monty Python's Flying Circus (1969–74)
    98

Morrissey Paul 23

Movie 3, 127, 128

'movie brats' 1, 4, 23

MTV Music Awards 111

Mulholland Dr. (2001) 119, 123–24,
    133–36, 154, 162
  production of (television pilot)
    136–41
  promotion and publicity campaigns
    for 142–51
  reception of 151–52

Mulvey, Laura 65, 72, 73, 75

My Hustler (1965) 22

Nana, Ed (*The Making of Dune*) 52,
    53, 58

Nance, Jack 24

National Review, The (review of *Blue
    Velvet*) 66

NBC (television network) 137

Neale, Steve 100

New Left Review 70

New Yorker 136

New York Times 90

Nichols, Mike 4

Nissan Micra car 118–19

Nochimson, Martha P. 43, 57, 60, 106,
    109–10

Northern Exposure (1990–95) 138

Ohlmeyer, Don 137

Ontkean, Michael 93

O'Reilly, Tim 45

Orvell, Miles 119

Ozu, Yasujiro 8, 64

Palme d'Or 102, 146

Parisienne cigarettes 118

Penn, Arthur 4

Pennsylvania Academy of Fine Arts
    (PAFA) 16

Perkins, Victor 127

Persona (1966) 151

Pevney, Joseph 128

Planet of the Apes franchise (1967–74)
    47, 159

Pleasure of the Text, The (Barthes) 38,
    40, 60–63

Plunderers, The (1960) 128

post-classical cinema 1, 2, 5, 14–15,
    90, 101, 108, 123, 125, 128,
    140–44, 148–49, 152, 155

postmodernism 4, 29, 31, 68–70,
73–74, 82, 95
post-structuralism 38, 43, 65, 72, 78,
135
Pourroy, Janine and Don Shay 47,
49
Premiere (magazine) 150
Pulp Fiction (1994) 32

Quart, Leonard and Albert Auster
3

Rafelson, Bob 4
Rafferty, Terrence 89, 92, 103
Raging Bull (1980) 31
Rainer, Yvonne 25
Rambaldi, Carlo 62
Return of the Jedi (1984) 49
Revue du Cinéma 3
Rezeptionsäesthetik 5, 9
Richter, Hans 34
Ringwood, Bob 52–53, 62
Roberts, Adam 45
Rocky Horror Picture Show, The (1975)
25
Rodley, Chris 48, 69, 109, 113, 116
Rosenbaum, Jonathan 24
Rossellini, Isabella 31
'Ruth, Roses and Revolvers: David
Lynch Presents the Surrealists'
33

Sammon, Paul D. 29
Sanders, Jill 113
Sarris, Andrew 2

Scorpio Rising (1963) 158
Scorsese, Martin 4, 112, 154
Scott, Ridley 48
Secret Diary of Laura Palmer, The
(*Twin Peaks* series tie-in book)
(1990) 97
Seydoux, Michael 47, 48
Shake Rattle and Roll (1956) 158
Shattuc, Jane M. 72–74
Shivas, Mark 127
Short Films of David Lynch, The (2002)
106
Singing Detective, The (1986) 98
Sirk, Douglas 7
Six Men Getting Sick (1967) 16, 106,
157
Smithee, Allen and Judas Booth 44,
159
Something Wild (1986) 71
Spielberg, Steven 4
Splet, Alan R. 28, 37
Staiger, Janet 2, 8, 11–12, 14–15,
19–22, 66, 75, 82, 95, 126,
133–34, 155, 158
Star Wars (1977) 24, 49
similarities with *Dune* 51–52
Straight Story, The (1999) 16, 108, 111,
123–24, 137, 150
Stranger in a Strange Land (novel)
(1961) 44
Stern, Lesley 67, 72–73
structuralism 43, 65, 69
StudioCanal/CanalPlus 123,
129, 131–32, 141, 143,
162

surrealism/surrealist 4, 33, 100, 102, 118
Sutherland, J.A. 44
Sweeny, Mary 123, 141, 144
S/Z (Barthes) 38, 40, 60–63

Tao, Steve 137–40
Tarantino, Quentin 4, 32
Technics 'Home Cinema Range' 112–14
teen-pix 21
Ten Commandments, The (1956) 57
textual historicity 5, 7, 42, 66, 133, 135, 143
That Obscure Object of Desire (1977) 151
Theroux, Justin 140
Third Place, The (Sony Playstation games console) (2000) 118
thirtysomething (1987–91) 96
Thompson, David 32–33
Thompson, Kristin and David Bordwell 23, 158
Thriller (Michael Jackson) (1982) 112
Time, October 1990 91
Tomashevskii, Boris 8
Tompkins, Jane 7
Tonight Show, The 149–50
Tornatore, Giuseppe 117
Touchstone Television 138
transcendental meditation 129
Tudor, Andrew 134–35

Twentieth Century Fox 29
Twin Peaks (1990) 1, 5, 16, 32, 73, 86, 101–3, 107–9, 136, 138, 146, 150, 160
affection for in Japan 161
cultural impact of 87–96
reception in the British press 92–99
Twin Peaks: Fire Walk with Me (1992) 16, 86–87, 100, 101, 103–7, 108, 132
negative critical reception of 103–5, 124, 128

Universal Pictures 29, 48–49, 54, 143, 150

Venice Film Festival 131
Vertigo (1958) 151
Vogel, Amos 21
Vogue 120
Vormittagsspuk (1928) 34

'Wall, The' (advertisement for German sportswear company Adidas) (1993) 117–18
Warhol, Andy 22
Wasteland (1999) 140
Waters, John 23, 25
Watts, Naomi 143–44, 150
Welcome to Twin Peaks (series tie-in book) (1991) 97
West, Kit 53
'What is an author?' (Foucault) 40

Wild at Heart (1990) 90, 100–3, 104,
110
Williamson, Judith 119
Wimsatt and Beardsley ('intentional
fallacy') 64
Wolfe, Gary K. 51
Wollen, Peter 122–23, 127–28, 135,
140, 141, 143
Woods, Paul A. 15, 57, 111

Wurlitzer, Rudolph 48
Wyatt, Justin 25–26

X-Files, The (1993–2002) 138

'yuppie' 96
Yves Saint Laurent 113

Zoglin, Richard 95